The Cove

Crochet Blanket by Shelley Husband

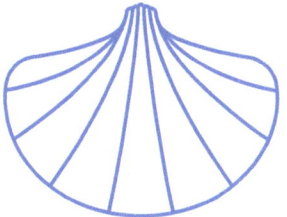

US Terms

Copyright © 2024 by Shelley Husband

All rights reserved. No part of this publication may be reproduced or transmitted by any means, electronic, photocopying or otherwise without prior written permission of the author.

ISBN: 978-0-6486053-1-7

Charts made by Amy Gunderson

Email: kinglouiespizza@gmail.com

Ravelry ID: AmyGunderson

Graphic Design by Michelle Lorimer

Email: hello@michellelorimer.com

Technical Editing by SiewBee Pond

Email: essbee1995@yahoo.com

Chart technical editing by Kelly Lonergan

Email: kelly@hazennainspired.com

Blanket Photography by Jo O'Keefe

Email: jookeefe@hotmail.com

Instagram: missfarmerjojo

Other Photography by Shelley Husband

First edition 2024

Published by Shelley Husband

PO Box 11

Narrawong VIC 3285

Australia

shelleyhusbandcrochet.com

0824

Contents

Explore The Cove • 05

What to Pack • 06

Map • 12

Paths to Explore • 13

    Coastal Sunrise • 14

    Reef Ripples • 16

    Seashells • 19

    Wickerwork • 24

    Cabana Days • 28

    Pebble Beach (Shortcut) • 36

Scenic Route • 40

    Sunset Shells • 42

    Ripples • 46

    Fans • 48

    Wicker • 52

    Pebble Beach (Scenic Route) • 54

Guide Book • 59

    Coastal Sunrise • 60

    Reef Ripples • 66

    Seashells • 78

    Wickerwork • 94

    Cabana Days • 102

    Pebble Beach • 126

Small Patterns • 132

    Sunset Shells • 132

    Ripples • 136

    Fans • 141

    Wicker • 146

Glossary • 150

Helpful Links • 152

Thank You • 153

About the Author • 154

Other Books by Shelley Husband • 155

Explore

The Cove

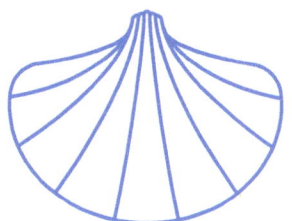

A pick your path pattern inspired by coastal adventures

Come with me as we explore the wonders of The Cove.

Admire the Coastal Sunrise from the cliff tops. Linger on the sandy shore to watch the ripples roll in over the reef. Collect a seashell as a memory of your sojourn. Relax with a cool drink in a wickerwork chair. Ponder the possibility of stopping for a new arrival. Laze in a beach-side cabana.

At the fork in the road, explore the scenic route to encounter fossils, a fern forest, a hidden lake, and a lookout to wonder at the view, or go directly to the end of the path to the stony, tactile beauty of Pebble Beach.

I'll be your guide along the way, keeping you on the path, helping you navigate the twists and turns.

I hope you enjoy your gentle trip around The Cove.

What to Pack

The Cove has many paths you can choose between.

I have listed the specifications of the yarn used for each sample shown.

You can use any yarn to create your Cove. Compare the metres per gram ratio of the yarn I used to the one you would like to use. If they are similar, the yarn amounts quoted here will be fine. If it differs, you will need more or less yarn and your finished piece will likely be a different size.

Coastal Sunrise Coaster

Bendigo Woollen Mills Cotton 8 ply
485 metres per 200-gram ball

Metres per gram: 2.425

Hook: 4.5 mm

Size: 10.5 cm/4.25 in across

Amount needed for 1 coaster: 10 grams

Colour used: Latte

Kym's Wickerwork Baby Blanket

Bendigo Woollen Mills Classic Wool 8 ply
400 metres per 200-gram ball

Metres per gram: 2

Hook: 4.5 mm

Size: 80 x 80 cm/31 x 31 in

Amount needed: 550 grams/3 balls

Colour used: Raffia

Shelley's Shortcut Lap Blanket

Bendigo Woollen Mills Cotton 8 ply
485 metres per 200-gram ball

Metres per gram: 2.425

Hook: 4.5 mm

Size: 130 x 130 cm/51 x 51 in

Amount needed: approx. 1,200 grams/6 or 7 balls

Colour used: Latte

Chris's Shortcut Lap Blanket

Drops Paris Uni Colour Cotton
75 metres per 50-gram ball

Metres per gram: 1.5

Hook: 5 mm

Size: 150 x 150 cm/59 x 59 in

Amount needed: approx. 2,400 grams/ 48 to 50 balls

Colour used: 58 Powder Pink

Shelley's Scenic Route Blanket

Bendigo Woollen Mills Cotton 8 ply
485 metres per 200-gram ball

Metres per gram: 2.425

Hook: 4.5 mm

Size: 180 x 180 cm/71 x 71 in

Amount needed: approx. 2,000 grams/10 or 11 balls

Colour used: Parchment

Kim's Scenic Route Blanket

Fiddlesticks WREN 8 ply cotton
125 metres per 50-gram ball

Metres per gram: 2.5

Hook: 3.5 mm

Size: 140 x 140 cm/55 x 55 in

Amounts and Colours:

- Ⓐ Ivory (W003): 550 grams/11 or 12 balls
- Ⓑ Butter (W004): 240 grams/6 balls
- Ⓒ Banana (W005): 200 grams/4 or 5 balls
- Ⓓ Stone (W019): 310 grams/7 balls
- Ⓔ Ice Blue (W023): 280 grams/6 or 7 balls
- Ⓕ Sky (W024): 230 grams/6 balls

The colours to use for each round are shown with icons in the written pattern. The icons for each colour are next to the yarn needs above.

Look to the end of the stitch count for the colour to use for that round.

Most of the time, you will be changing colour each round, but there are a few instances where the same colour is used for 2 to 4 rounds.

What to Pack

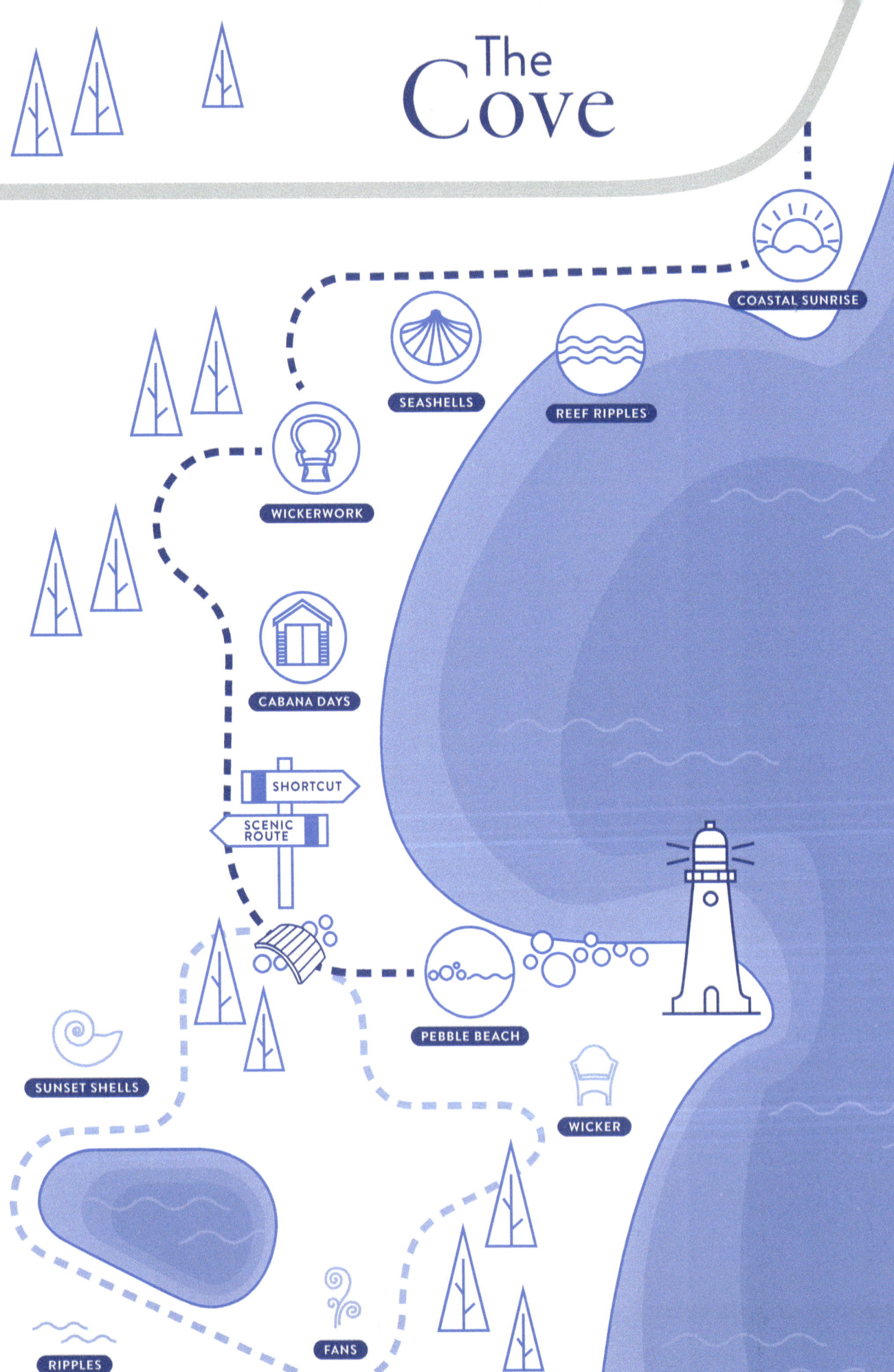

Paths to Explore

The path around The Cove begins at the top of the cliffs with the Coastal Sunrise. How far along the path you go is up to you.

Here are the possible pathways.

Coastal Sunrise Coaster Directions

Make Rounds 1 – 5.

For a seamless edge, change Round 6 to:

ch1, *2sc in 1-ch sp, skip 1 st, 2sc in 1-ch sp**, sc in next st*, rep from * to *10x & * to ** 1x, join with inv join to first true st. {60 sts}

Wickerwork Baby Blanket Directions

End Round 54 with chain 2, join with a slip stitch to first stitch.

The edges may be curling up. Blocking will make it sit flat.

Short Cut to Pebble Beach Lap Blanket

End Round 79 with chain 1, join with single crochet to first stitch and go directly to the Pebble Beach Shortcut Border pattern.

If you have yarn left over, consider extending the pebbles as Chris did by repeating Rounds 86 and 87 as many times as you wish before ending with Round 88.

Scenic Route Blanket

End at Round 79.

Make 8 Sunset Shells, Fans and Ripples squares and make 4 Wicker squares.

Join them per the schematic on page 41 into strips then to the centre panel.

Add the Pebble Beach Scenic Route Border pattern.

If you have left over yarn, consider extending the pebbles by repeating Rounds 87 and 88 as many times as you wish before ending with Round 89.

The Guide Book to help you navigate unfamiliar paths begins on page 59.

Coastal Sunrise

Rounds 1 - 6

Find the chart on page 15

Find the Round by Round Help on page 60

Begin with mc.

R1: ch3 (stch), 2dc around stch, *dc, 2dc around dc just made*, rep from * to * 6x, join with ss to 3rd ch of stch.
{24 sts}

R2: sc in same st as ss, sc in next 23 sts, join with ss to first st.
{24 sts}

R3: ch3 (stch), *2dc in next st**, dc in next st*, rep from * to * 10x & * to ** 1x, join with ss to 3rd ch of stch.
{36 sts}

R4: sc in same st as ss, *ch2, fpss around next 2 sts, ch2**, sc in next st*, rep from * to * 10x & * to ** 1x, join with ss to first st.
{36 sts, 24 2-ch sps}

R5: **Note: "dc4tog over next 2 sts" – begin 2 sts in each st**

sc in same st as ss, *ch1, dc4tog over next 2 sts of R3, ch1, skip (2-ch sp, 2 sts & 2-ch sp)**, sc in next st*, rep from * to * 10x & * to ** 1x, join with ss to first st.
{24 sts, 24 1-ch sps}

R6: sc in same st as ss, *2sc in 1-ch sp, skip 1 st, 2sc in 1-ch sp**, sc in next st*, rep from * to * 10x & * to ** 1x, join with ss to first st.
{60 sts}

If making a coaster, for a seamless edge, change R6 to:

ch1, *2sc in 1-ch sp, skip 1 st, 2sc in 1-ch sp**, sc in next st*, rep from * to *10x & * to ** 1x, join with inv join to first true st. {60 sts}

Coastal Sunrise
Right-handed chart

Coastal Sunrise

Reef Ripples

Rounds 7 - 20

Find the chart on page 17

Find the Round by Round Help on page 66

R7: ch3 (stch), dc in next 59 sts, join with ss to 3rd ch of stch.
{60 sts} D

R8: sc between same st as ss and next st, *sc between next 2 sts*, rep from * to * 58x, join with ss to first st.
{60 sts} A

R9: sc in same st as ss, *skip 2 sts, (2dc, ch1, 5dc, ch1, 2dc) in next st, skip 2 sts**, sc in next st*, rep from * to * 8x & * to ** 1x, join with ss to first st.
{100 sts, 20 1-ch sps} E

R10: ch3 (stch), 4dccl in same st as ss, *ch1, dc in next 2 sts, sc in both 1-ch sps either side of next 5 sts at the same time, dc in next 2 sts, ch1**, 5dccl in next st*, rep from * to * 8x & * to ** 1x, join with ss to top of 4dccl.
{60 sts, 20 1-ch sps} B

R11: sc in same st as ss, *sc in 1-ch sp, sc in next 5 sts, sc in 1-ch sp**, sc in next st*, rep from * to * 8x & * to ** 1x, join with ss to first st.
{80 sts} C

R12: *fpdc around R10 st below, ch2, bpdc around next 2 sts of R10, fpdc around next st of R10, bpdc around next 2 sts of R10, ch2*, rep from * to * 9x, join with ss to first st.
{60 sts, 20 2-ch sps} F

R13: sc in same st as ss, *2sc in 2-ch sp, sc in next 5 sts, 2sc in 2-ch sp**, sc in next st*, rep from * to * 8x & * to ** 1x, join with ss to first st.
{100 sts} D

R14: sc in same st as ss, *ch2, skip 4 sts, 7tr in next st, ch2, skip 4 sts**, sc in next st*, rep from * to * 8x & * to ** 1x, join with ss to first st.
{80 sts, 20 2-ch sps} A

Reef Ripples
Right-handed chart

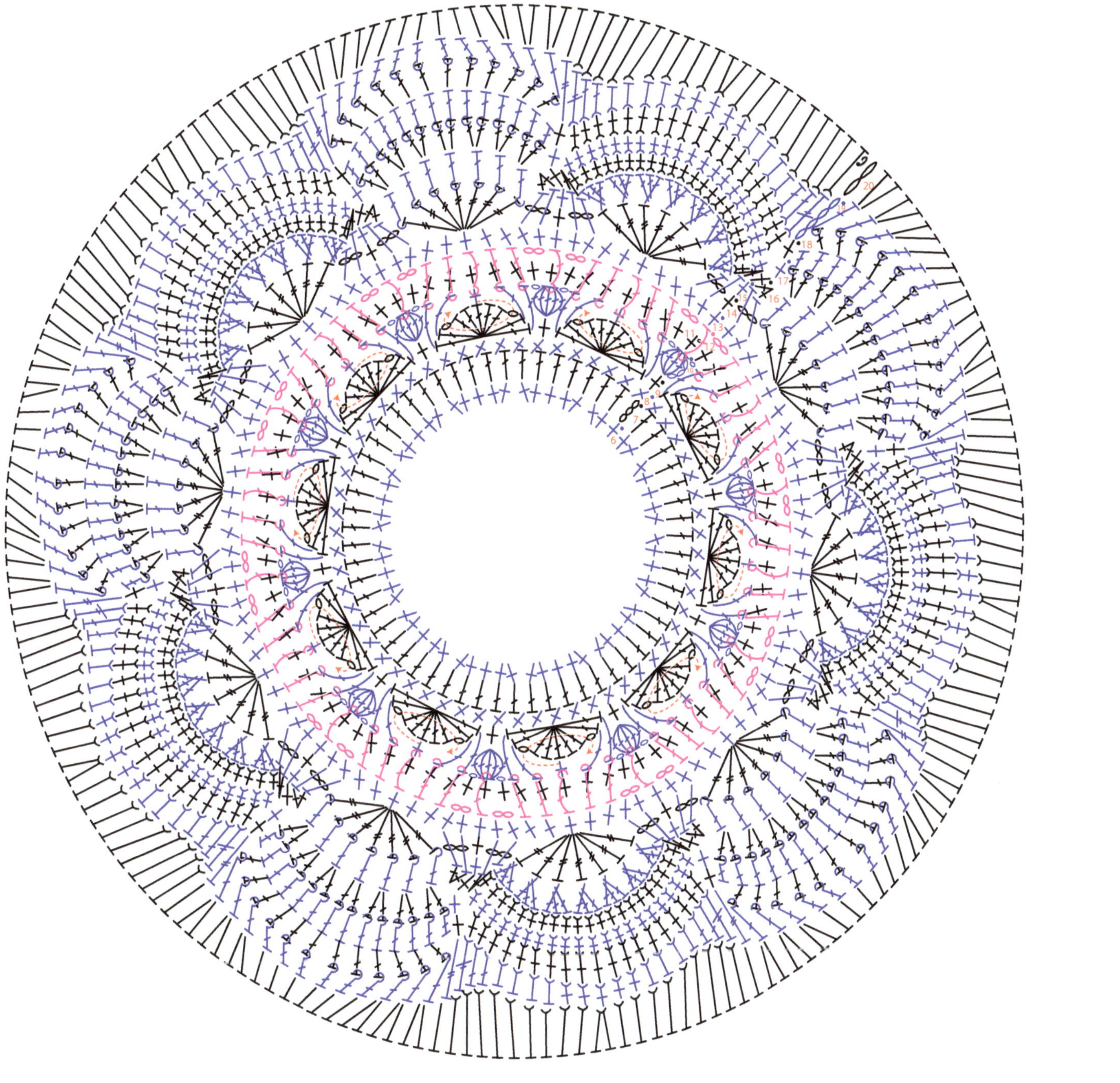

R15: sc in same st as ss, *hdc over 2-ch sp in each of the first 2 of 4 skipped sts of R13, 7x [dc in next st, 2dc around dc just made], hdc over 2-ch sp in each of the last 2 of 4 skipped sts of R13, sc in next st, hdc over 2-ch sp in each of the first 2 of 4 skipped sts of R13, bpdc around next 7 sts, hdc over 2-ch sp in each of the last 2 of 4 skipped sts of R13**, sc in next st*, rep from * to * 3x & * to ** 1x, join with ss to first st.
{190 sts}

R16: sc in same st as ss, *sc2tog over next 2 sts, sc in blo of next 21 sts, sc2tog over next 2 sts, sc in next st, sc2tog over next 2 sts, 2dc in next 7 sts, sc2tog over next 2 sts**, sc in next st*, rep from * to * 3x & * to ** 1x, join with ss to first st.
{205 sts}

R17: sc in same st as ss, *skip 1 st, sc in blo of next 21 sts, skip 1 st, sc in next st, skip 1 st, bpdc around next 14 sts, skip 1 st**, sc in next st*, rep from * to * 3x & * to ** 1x, join with ss to first st.
{185 sts}

R18: sc in same st as ss, *skip 1 st, sc in blo of next 19 sts, skip 1 st, sc in next st, skip 1 st, dc in next 12 sts, skip 1 st**, sc in next st*, rep from * to * 3x & * to ** 1x, join with ss to first st.
{165 sts}

R19: ch4 (stch), *htr in blo of next st, dc in blo of next 2 sts, hdc in blo of next 4 sts, sc in blo of next 5 sts, hdc in blo of next 4 sts, dc in blo of next 2 sts, htr in blo of next st, tr in next st, bpdc around next 12 sts**, tr in next st*, rep from * to * 3x & * to ** 1x, join with ss to 4th ch of stch.
{165 sts}

R20: ch2 (stch), *hdc in blo of next 9 sts, 2hdc in blo of next st, hdc in blo of next 9 sts, hdc in next st, 2hdc in next 3 sts, hdc in next 6 sts, 2hdc in next 3 sts**, hdc in next st*, rep from * to * 3x & * to ** 1x, join with inv join to first true st.
{200 sts}

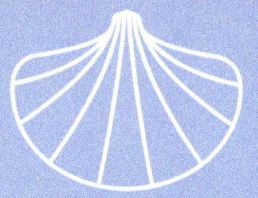

Seashells
Rounds 21 - 35

Find the chart on page 21

Find the Round by Round Help on page 78

R21: Attach with stdg dc to lbv of any stitch above a dip, dc in lbv of next 199 sts, join with ss to first st.
{200 sts}

R22: ch4 (stch), tr in same st as ss, *2tr in next st, 3tr in next st, skip 3 sts, sc in next 2 sts, 12x [dc in next st, 3dc around dc just made, skip 1 st, sc in next st], sc in next st, skip 3 sts, 3tr in next st, 2tr in next st**, 3tr in next st*, rep from * to * 2x & * to ** 1x, tr in same st as first sts, join with ss to 4th ch of stch.
{73 sts on each side; 4 3-st cnrs}

R23: ch4 (stch), fptr around same st as ss, *(tr in, fptr around) next 6 sts, skip 2 sts, 11x [bpdc around next st, ch2, skip 4 sts], bpdc around next st, skip 5 sts, (fptr around, tr in) next 6 sts**, (fptr around, tr in, fptr around) next st*, rep from * to * 2x & * to ** 1x, fptr around same st as first fp st, join with ss to 4th ch of stch.
{36 sts, 11 2-ch sps on each side; 4 3-st cnrs}

R24: sc in same st as ss, *sc in next 9 sts, sc2tog over next 2 sts, skip 3 sts, sc in lbv of first of 3dc around dc of R22, 11x [2dc in 2-ch sp, sc in lbv of first of 3dc around dc of R22, skip 1 st], skip 2 sts, sc2tog over next 2 sts, sc in next 9 sts**, sc in next st*, rep from * to * 2x & * to ** 1x, join with ss to first st.
{54 sts on each side; 4 1-st cnrs}

R25: ch3 (stch), dc in same st as ss, *dc in blo of next 10 sts, dc4tog over next 4 sts, 13x [skip 1 st, 2dc in next st, 2dc in skipped st], dc4tog over next 4 sts, dc in blo of next 10 sts**, 3dc in next st*, rep from * to * 2x & * to ** 1x, dc in same st as first sts, join with ss to 3rd ch of stch.
{74 sts on each side; 4 3-st cnrs}

R26: sc in same st as ss, *sc in blo of next 11 sts, skip 1 st, 13x [sc between last and next sts, ch2, skip 4 sts], sc between last and next sts, skip 1 st, sc in blo of next 11 sts**, (sc, ch2, sc) in next st*, rep from * to * 2x & * to ** 1x, sc in same st as first st, ch1, join with sc to first st.
{38 sts, 13 2-ch sps on each side; 4 2-ch cnr sps} C

R27: sc over joining sc, *6x [ch1, skip 1 st, sc in next st], sc in next st, 6x [5dc in 2-ch sp, skip 1 st, sc in 2-ch sp, skip 1 st], 5dc in 2-ch sp, sc in next st, 6x [sc in next st, ch1, skip 1 st]**, sc in 2-ch cnr sp*, rep from * to * 2x & * to ** 1x, join with ss to first st.
{55 sts, 12 1-ch sps on each side; 4 1-st cnrs} A

R28: **puff – 3x [yo, insert in sp, pull up loop], yo, pull through all loops**

ch3 (stch), *6x [puff in 1-ch sp, dc in next st], skip 1 st, sc in lbv of next 2 sts, 6x [sc in lbv of next st, skip 2 sts, 5dc in next st, skip 2 sts], sc in lbv of next 3 sts, skip 1 st, 6x [dc in next st, puff in 1-ch sp]**, dc in next st*, rep from * to * 2x & * to ** 1x, join with ss to 3rd ch of stch.
{65 sts on each side; 4 1-st cnrs} E

R29: sc in same st as ss, *6x [(sc in, fpsc around) next st, sc in next st], skip 1 st, sc in next 2 sts, sc in lbv of next 2 sts, 5x [sc in lbv of next st, skip 2 sts, 5dc in next st, skip 2 sts], sc in lbv of next 3 sts, sc in next 2 sts, skip 1 st, 6x [sc in next st, (sc in, fpsc around) next st]**, (sc, ch2, sc) in next st*, rep from * to * 2x & * to ** 1x, sc in same st as first st, ch1, join with sc to first st.
{77 sts on each side; 4 2-ch cnr sps} D

R30: ch3 (stch), *dc in blo of next 19 sts, skip 2 sts, sc in next 3 sts, sc in lbv of next 2 sts, 4x [sc in lbv of next st, skip 2 sts, 5dc in next st, skip 2 sts], sc in lbv of next 3 sts, sc in next 3 sts, skip 2 sts, dc in blo of next 19 sts**, dc in 2-ch cnr sp*, rep from * to * 2x & * to ** 1x, join with ss to 3rd ch of stch.
{73 sts on each side; 4 1-st cnrs} C

R31: sc in same st as ss, *sc in blo of next 19 sts, skip 1 st, sc in next 5 sts, sc in lbv of next 2 sts, 3x [sc in lbv of next st, skip 2 sts, 5dc in next st, skip 2 sts], sc in lbv of next 3 sts, sc in next 5 sts, skip 1 st, sc in blo of next 19 sts**, (sc, ch2, sc) in next st*, rep from * to * 2x & * to ** 1x, sc in same st as first st, ch1, join with sc to first st.
{73 sts on each side; 4 2-ch cnr sps} F

Seashells
Right-handed chart

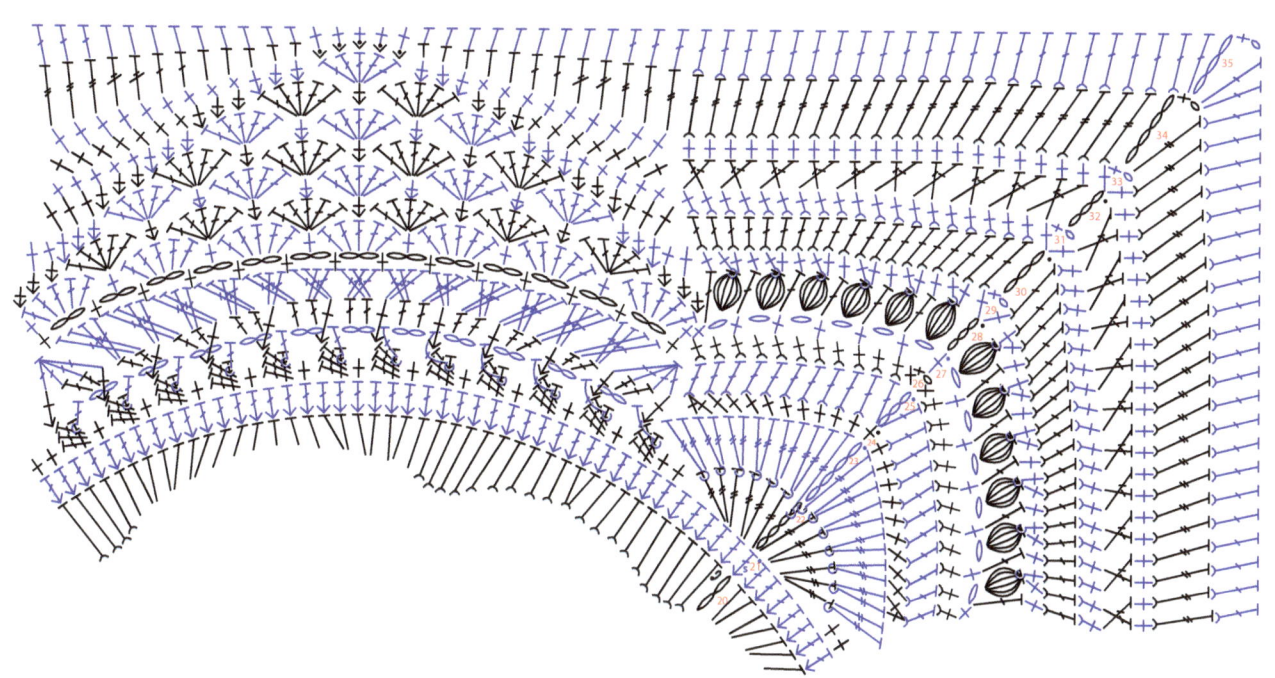

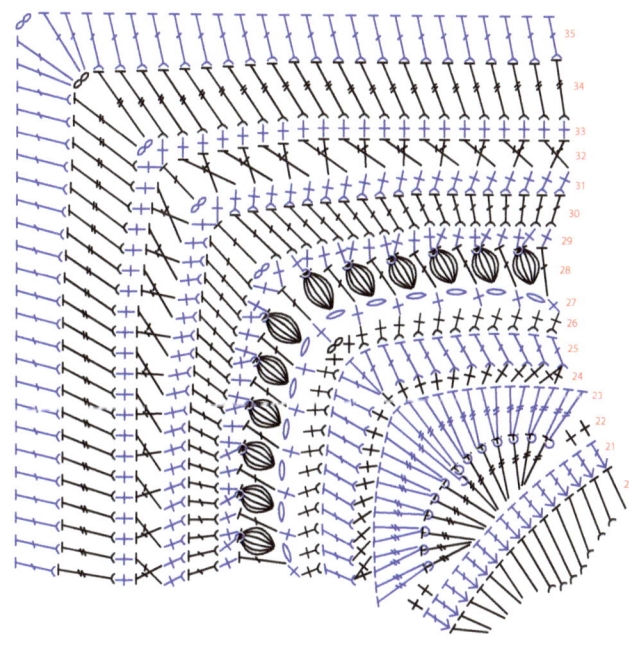

R32: ch3 (stch), *10x [skip 1 st, dc in next st, dc in skipped st], skip 1 st, sc in next 7 sts, sc in lbv of next 2 sts, 2x [sc in lbv of next st, skip 2 sts, 5dc in next st, skip 2 sts], sc in lbv of next 3 sts, sc in next 7 sts, skip 1 st, 10x [skip 1 st, dc in next st, dc in skipped st]**, dc in 2-ch cnr sp*, rep from * to * 2x & * to ** 1x, join with ss to 3rd ch of stch.
{71 sts on each side; 4 1-st cnrs} E

R33: sc in same st as ss, *sc in next 20 sts, skip 1 st, sc in next 9 sts, sc in lbv of next 3 sts, skip 2 sts, 5dc in next st, skip 2 sts, sc in lbv of next 3 sts, sc in next 9 sts, skip 1 st, sc in next 20 sts**, (sc, ch2, sc) in next st*, rep from * to * 2x & * to ** 1x, sc in same st as first st, ch1, join with sc to first st.
{71 sts on each side; 4 2-ch cnr sps} D

R34: ch4 (stch), *tr in blo of next 21 sts, tr in next 3 sts, htr in next 2 sts, dc in next 2 sts, hdc in next 5 sts, ss in lbv of next 5 sts, hdc in next 5 sts, dc in next 2 sts, htr in next 2 sts, tr in next 3 sts, tr in blo of next 21 sts**, (tr, ch2, tr) in 2-ch cnr sp*, rep from * to * 2x & * to ** 1x, tr in same sp as first st, ch1, join with sc to 4th ch of stch.
{73 sts on each side; 4 2-ch cnr sps} A

R35: ch3 (stch), dc over joining sc, *dc in blo of next 22 sts, dc in next 3 sts, hdc in next 9 sts, sc in blo of next 5 sts, hdc in next 9 sts, dc in next 3 sts, dc in blo of next 22 sts**, (2dc, ch2, 2dc) in 2-ch cnr sp*, rep from * to * 2x & * to ** 1x, 2dc in same sp as first sts, ch1, join with sc to 3rd ch of stch.
{77 sts on each side; 4 2-ch cnr sps} A

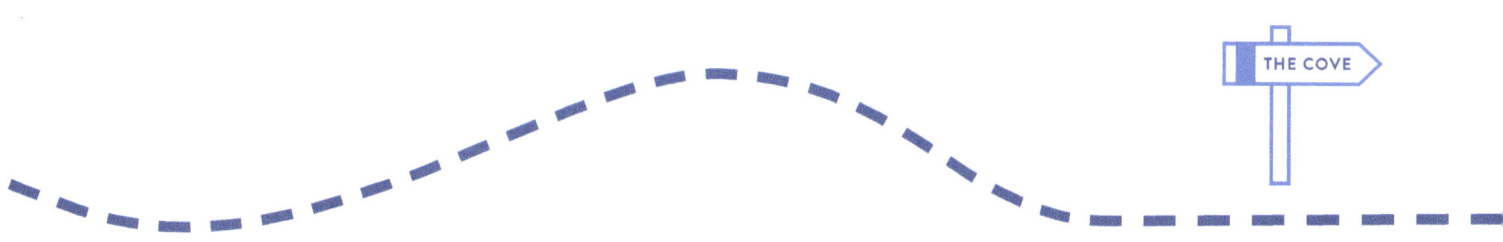

Seashells

23

Wickerwork
Rounds 36 - 54

Find the chart on page 26

Find the Round by Round Help on page 94

R36: sc over joining sc, *sc in blo of next 77 sts**, (sc, ch2, sc) in 2-ch cnr sp*, rep from * to * 2x & * to ** 1x, sc in same sp as first st, ch1, join with sc to first st.
{79 sts on each side; 4 2-ch cnr sps} Ⓐ

R37: ch3 (stch), 2dc over joining sc, *ch2, skip 1 st, 26x [dc4tog over next 3 sts skipping the middle st with 2 legs in each st, ch2]**, (2dc, htr, 2dc) in 2-ch cnr sp*, rep from * to * 2x & * to ** 1x, 2dc in same sp as first sts, join with ss to 3rd ch of stch.
{26 sts, 27 2-ch sps on each side; 4 5-st cnrs} Ⓑ

R38: sc in same st as ss, *sc in next 2 sts, 26x [2sc in 2-ch sp, spike sc over next st into skipped st of R36], 2sc in 2-ch sp, sc in next 2 sts**, (sc, ch2, sc) in next st*, rep from * to * 2x & * to ** 1x, sc in same st as first st, ch1, join with sc to first st.
{86 sts on each side; 4 2-ch cnr sps} Ⓒ

R39: ch3 (stch), dc over joining sc, *skip 1 st, dc in next 85 sts**, (dc, htr, dc) in 2-ch cnr sp*, rep from * to * 2x & * to ** 1x, dc in same sp as first sts, join with ss to 3rd ch of stch.
{85 sts on each side; 4 3-st cnrs} Ⓐ

R40: sc in same st as ss, *sc in next 87 sts**, (sc, ch2, sc) in next st*, rep from * to * 2x & * to ** 1x, sc in same st as first st, ch1, join with sc to first st.
{89 sts on each side; 4 2-ch cnr sps} Ⓐ

R41: ch3 (stch), *17x [ch2, dc4tog over next 4 sts, ch2, sc in next st], ch2, dc4tog over next 4 sts, ch2**, dc in 2-ch cnr sp*, rep from * to * 2x & * to ** 1x, join with ss to 3rd ch of stch.
{35 sts, 36 2-ch sps on each side; 4 1-st cnrs} Ⓕ

R42: ch3 (stch), 2dc in same st as ss, *skip 2-ch sp, 17x [sc in next st, skip 2-ch sp, 4dc in next st, skip 2-ch sp], sc in next st, skip 2-ch sp**, 5dc in next st*, rep from * to * 2x & * to ** 1x, 2dc in same st as first sts, join with ss to 3rd ch of stch.
{86 sts on each side; 4 5-st cnrs} Ⓔ

Wickerwork

R43: sc in same st as ss, *sc in next 2 sts, 17x [ch2, fpdc around next R41 st, ch2, bpdc around next R41 st], ch2, fpdc around next R41 st, ch2, skip all sts until last 2, sc in last 2 sts**, (sc, ch2, sc) in next st*, rep from * to * 2x & * to ** 1x, sc in same st as first st, ch1, join with sc to first st.
{41 sts, 36 2-ch sps on each side; 4 2-ch cnr sps} F

R44: sc over joining sc, *sc in next 3 sts, 35x [2sc in 2-ch sp, sc in next st], 2sc in 2-ch sp, sc in next 3 sts**, (sc, ch2, sc) in 2-ch cnr sp*, rep from * to * 2x & * to ** 1x, sc in same sp as first st, ch1, join with sc to first st.
{115 sts on each side; 4 2-ch cnr sps} D

R45: ch3 (stch), dc over joining sc, *skip 1 st, dc in next 114 sts**, 3dc in 2-ch cnr sp*, rep from * to * 2x & * to ** 1x, dc in same sp as first sts, join with ss to 3rd ch of stch.
{114 sts on each side; 4 3-st cnrs} A

R46: sc in same st as ss, *sc in next 116 sts**, (sc, ch2, sc) in next st*, rep from * to * 2x & * to ** 1x, sc in same st as first st, ch1, join with sc to first st.
{118 sts on each side; 4 2-ch cnr sps} D

R47: ch3 (stch), dc over joining sc, *skip 1 st, dc in next 117 sts**, 3dc in 2-ch cnr sp*, rep from * to * 2x & * to ** 1x, dc in same sp as first sts, join with ss to 3rd ch of stch.
{117 sts on each side; 4 3-st cnrs} C

R48: ch3 (stch), dc in same st as ss, *59x [dc in next st, fpdc around next st], dc in next st**, 3dc in next st*, rep from * to * 2x & * to ** 1x, dc in same st as first sts, join with ss to 3rd ch of stch.
{119 sts on each side; 4 3-st cnrs} E

R49: ch3 (stch), dc in same st as ss, *60x [dc in next st, fpdc around next st], dc in next st**, 3dc in next st*, rep from * to * 2x & * to ** 1x, dc in same st as first sts, join with ss to 3rd ch of stch.
{121 sts on each side; 4 3-st cnrs} A

R50: ch3 (stch), dc in same st as ss, *61x [dc in next st, fpdc around next st], dc in next st**, 3dc in next st*, rep from * to * 2x & * to ** 1x, dc in same st as first sts, join with ss to 3rd ch of stch.
{123 sts on each side; 4 3-st cnrs} E

R51: ch3 (stch), dc in same st as ss, *62x [dc in next st, fpdc around next st], dc in next st**, 3dc in next st*, rep from * to * 2x & * to ** 1x, dc in same st as first sts, join with ss to 3rd ch of stch.
{125 sts on each side; 4 3-st cnrs} C

Note: It will be curling up at this point.

Wickerwork
Right-handed chart

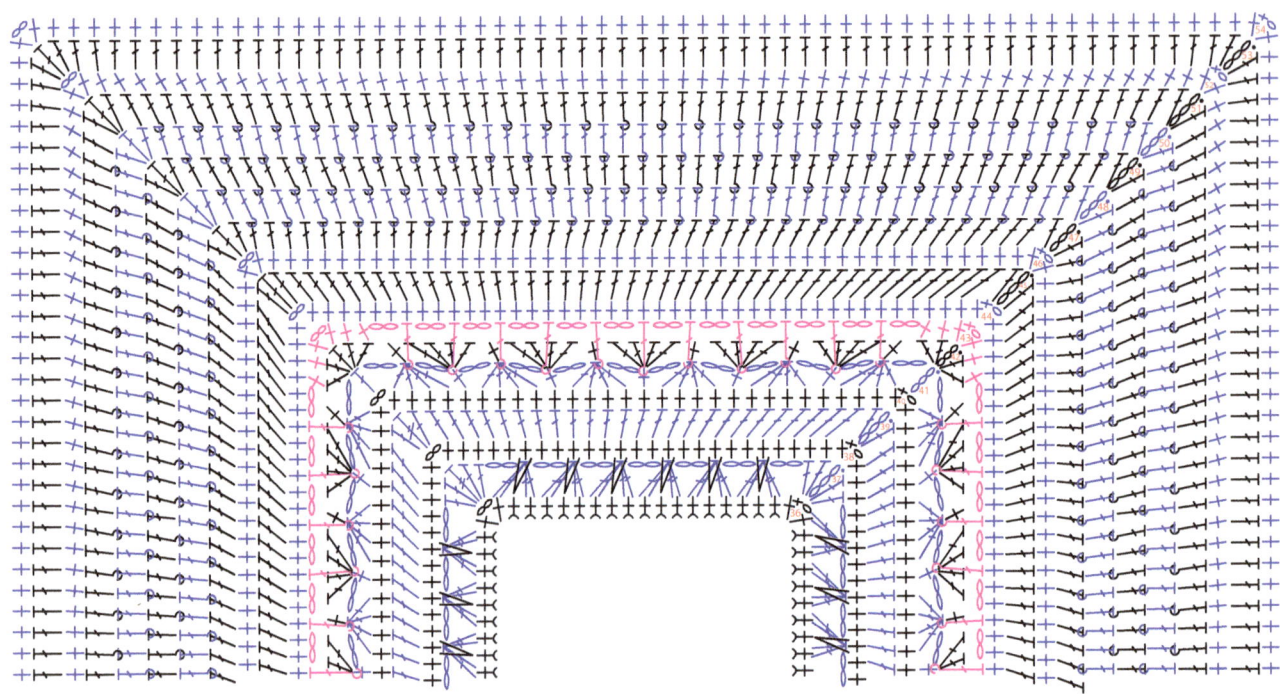

- **R52:** sc in same st as ss, *sc in next 127 sts**, (sc, ch2, sc) in next st*, rep from * to * 2x & * to ** 1x, sc in same st as first st, ch1, join with sc to first st.
{129 sts on each side; 4 2-ch cnr sps} D

- **R53:** ch3 (stch), dc over joining sc, *dc in next 129 sts**, 3dc in 2-ch cnr sp*, rep from * to * 2x & * to ** 1x, dc in same sp as first sts, join with ss to 3rd ch of stch.
{129 sts on each side; 4 3-st cnrs} A

- **R54:** sc in same st as ss, *sc in next 131 sts**, (sc, ch2, sc) in next st*, rep from * to * 2x & * to ** 1x, sc in same st as first st, ch1, join with sc to first st.
{133 sts on each side; 4 2-ch cnr sps} D

If making the Wickerwork Baby Blanket, end Round 54 with ch2, join with a ss to first st.

The edges may be curling up. Blocking will make it sit flat.

Wickerwork

Cabana Days
Rounds 55 - 79

Find the chart on page 29

Find the Round by Round Help on page 102

R55: ch3 (stch), *66x [skip 1 st, (dc, ch1, dc) in next st], skip 1 st** (dc, ch1, dc) in 2-ch cnr sp*, rep from * to * 2x & * to ** 1x, dc in same sp as first st, join with sc to 3rd ch of stch.
{134 sts on each side; 4 1-ch cnr sps} E

R56: ch3 (stch), dc over joining sc, *fpdc around next st, 66x [ch1, fpdc2tog over next 2 sts skipping the 1-ch sp], ch1, fpdc around next st**, 3dc in 1-ch cnr sp*, rep from * to * 2x & * to ** 1x, dc in same sp as first sts, join with ss to 3rd ch of stch.
{68 sts, 67 1-ch sps on each side; 4 3-st cnrs} F

R57: ch3 (stch), dc in same st as ss, *fpdc around next 2 sts, 66x [sc in 1-ch sp, tr in skipped st of R54 behind, fpsc around next st], sc in 1-ch sp, tr in skipped st of R54 behind, fpdc around next 2 sts**, 3dc in next st*, rep from * to * 2x & * to ** 1x, dc in same st as first sts, join with ss to 3rd ch of stch.
{204 sts on each side; 4 3-st cnrs} A

R58: sc in same st as ss, *sc in next 3 sts, 33x [sc2tog over next 2 sts, skip next st, sc2tog over next 2 sts, sc in next st], sc2tog over next 2 sts, sc in next 3 sts**, (sc, ch2, sc) in next st*, rep from * to * 2x & * to ** 1x, sc in same st as first st, ch1, join with sc to first st.
{108 sts on each side; 4 2-ch cnr sps} A

R59: sc over joining sc, *skip 1 st, 2x [fptr around next fp st of R57, dc in next st], hdc in next 103 sts, 2x [dc in next st, fptr around next fp st of R57 below]**, sc in 2-ch cnr sp*, rep from * to * 2x & * to ** 1x, join with ss to first st.
{111 sts on each side; 4 1-st cnrs} A

R60: skip same st as ss, fpdc around 2 fp sts either side of the cnr below at the same time, *2dc in next st, (fpdc around, 2dc in) next st, dc in next st, hdc in lbv of next 103 sts, dc in next st, (2dc in, fpdc around) next st, 2dc in next st**, fpdc around 2 fp sts either side of the cnr below at the same time skipping the st between*, rep from * to * 2x & * to ** 1x, join with ss to first st.
{115 sts on each side; 4 1-st cnrs} B

Cabana Days
Right-handed chart

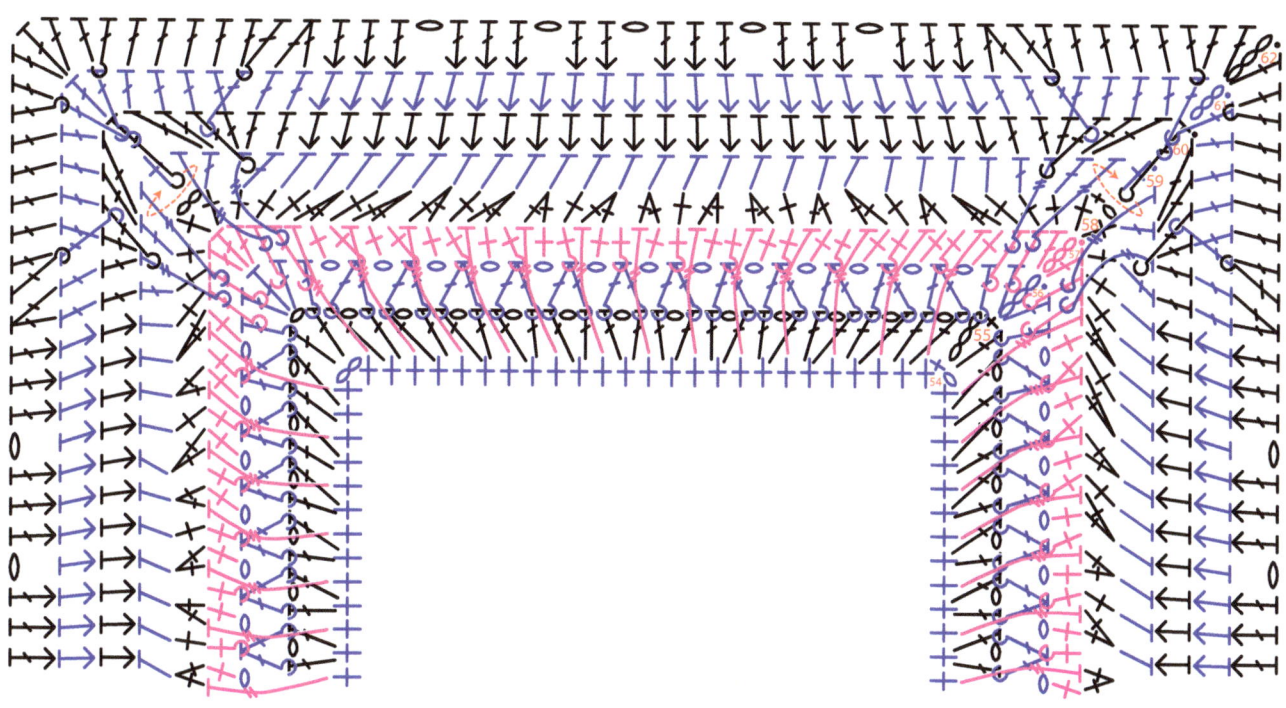

R61: ch3 (stch), fpdc around same st as ss, *dc in next 4 sts, fpdc around fp to the right, dc in next 2 sts, hdc in lbv of next 103 sts, dc in next 2 sts, fpdc around fp to the left, dc in next 4 sts**, (fpdc around, dc in, fpdc around) next st*, rep from * to * 2x & * to ** 1x, fpdc around same st as first sts, join with ss to 3rd ch of stch.
{117 sts on each side; 4 3-st cnrs} **E**

R62: ch3 (stch), dc in same st as ss, *(dc in, fpdc around) next st, dc in next 4 sts, (dc in, fpdc around) next st, dc2tog over next 2 sts, 25x [dc in lbv of next 3 sts, ch1, skip 1 st], dc in lbv of next 3 sts, dc2tog over next 2 sts, (fpdc around, dc in) next st, dc in next 4 sts, (fpdc around, dc in) next st**, 3dc in next st*, rep from * to ^ 2x & * to ** 1x, dc in same st as first sts, join with ss to 3rd ch of stch.
{96 sts, 25 1-ch sps along each side; 4 3-st cnrs} **F**

R63: sc in same st as ss, sc in next 2 sts, *fphdc around next st, bpdc around next 5 sts, fpdc around next st, skip 1 st, sc in next st, fpsc around next st, 25x [skip 1 st, 5dc in 1-ch sp, skip 1 st, fpsc around next st], sc in next st, skip 1 st, fpdc around next st, bpdc around next 5 sts, fphdc around next st**, sc in next 5 sts*, rep from * to * 2x & * to ** 1x, sc in next 2 sts, join with ss to first st.
{171 sts on each side; 4 1-st cnrs} D

R64: sc in same st as ss, *sc in next 10 sts, 25x [fpsc around next st, 3tr in lbv of skipped st of R61 behind, skip 5 sts], fpsc around next st, sc in next 10 sts**, (sc, ch2, sc) in next st*, rep from * to * 2x & * to ** 1x, sc in same st as first st, ch1, join with sc to first st.
{123 sts on each side; 4 2-ch cnr sps} C

R65: **Note: Don't work a false st.** ch3 (stch), dc over joining sc, *dc in next 4 sts, bpdc around next 5 R63 sts, skip 5 sts, sc in next 2 sts, 25x [ss in next st, 2hdc in next st, 3hdc in next st, 2hdc in next st], ss in next st, sc in next 2 sts, bpdc around next 5 R63 sts, skip 5 sts, dc in next 4 sts**, 3dc in 2-ch cnr sp*, rep from * to * 2x & * to ** 1x, dc in same sp as first sts, join with inv join to first true st.
{223 sts on each side; 4 3-st cnrs} G

R66: Attach with stdg bpdc to the middle st of any 3-st cnr, bpdc around next 5 sts, *sc in next 7 sts, skip 1 st, 12x [sc in lbv of next 7 sts, bpdc around next 3 sts of R64, skip 9 sts], sc in lbv of next 7 sts, skip 1 st, sc in next 7 sts**, bpdc around next 11 sts*, rep from * to * 2x & * to ** 1x, bpdc around next 5 sts, join with ss to first st.
{141 sts on each side; 4 11-st cnrs} A

R67: **Note: The 6tog are worked with 2 legs in 3 sts.**

ch3 (stch), dc in same st as ss, *dc in next 19 sts, 11x [ch1, tr6tog over next 3 sts, ch1, dc in next 7 sts], ch1, tr6tog over next 3 sts, ch1, dc in next 19 sts**, 3dc in next st*, rep from * to * 2x & * to ** 1x, dc in same st as first sts, join with ss to 3rd ch of stch.
{127 sts, 24 1-ch sps on each side; 4 3-st cnrs} A

R68: sc in same st as ss, *sc in next 20 sts, 11x [skip 1-ch sp, fpsc around next st, skip 1-ch sp, sc in next 7 sts], skip 1-ch sp, fpsc around next st, skip 1-ch sp, sc in next 20 sts**, (sc, ch2, sc) in next st*, rep from * to * 2x & * to ** 1x, sc in same st as first st, ch1, join with sc to first st.
{131 sts on each side; 4 2-ch cnr sps} A

R69: sc over joining sc, *sc in next 131 sts**, (sc, ch2, sc) in 2-ch cnr sp*, rep from * to * 2x & * to ** 1x, sc in same sp as first st, ch1, join with sc to first st.
{133 sts on each side; 4 2-ch cnr sps} A

Cabana Days
Right-handed chart

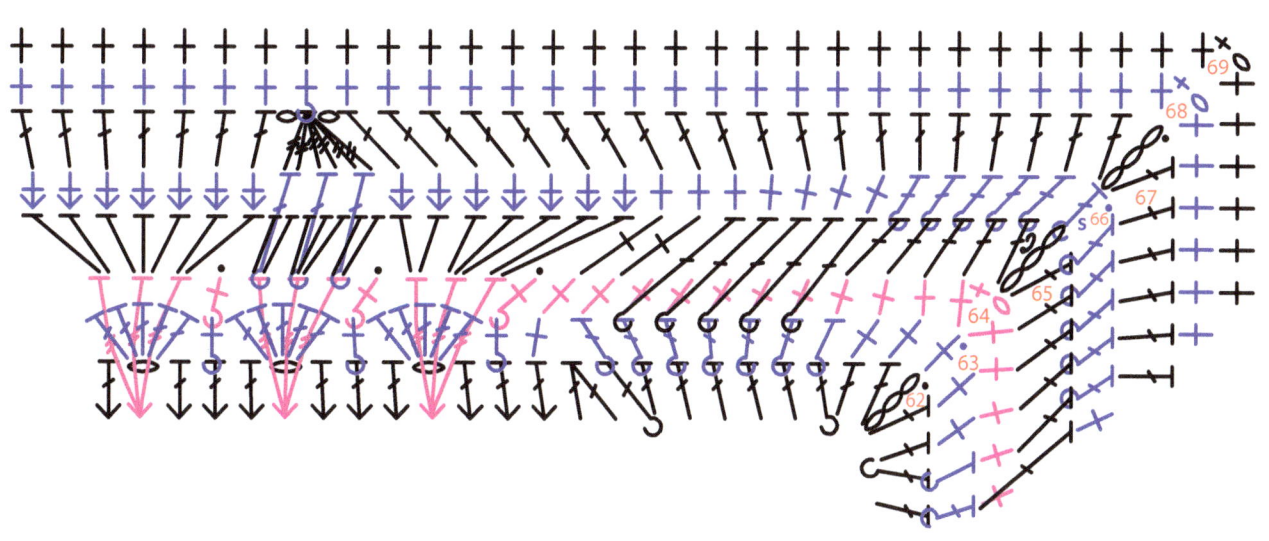

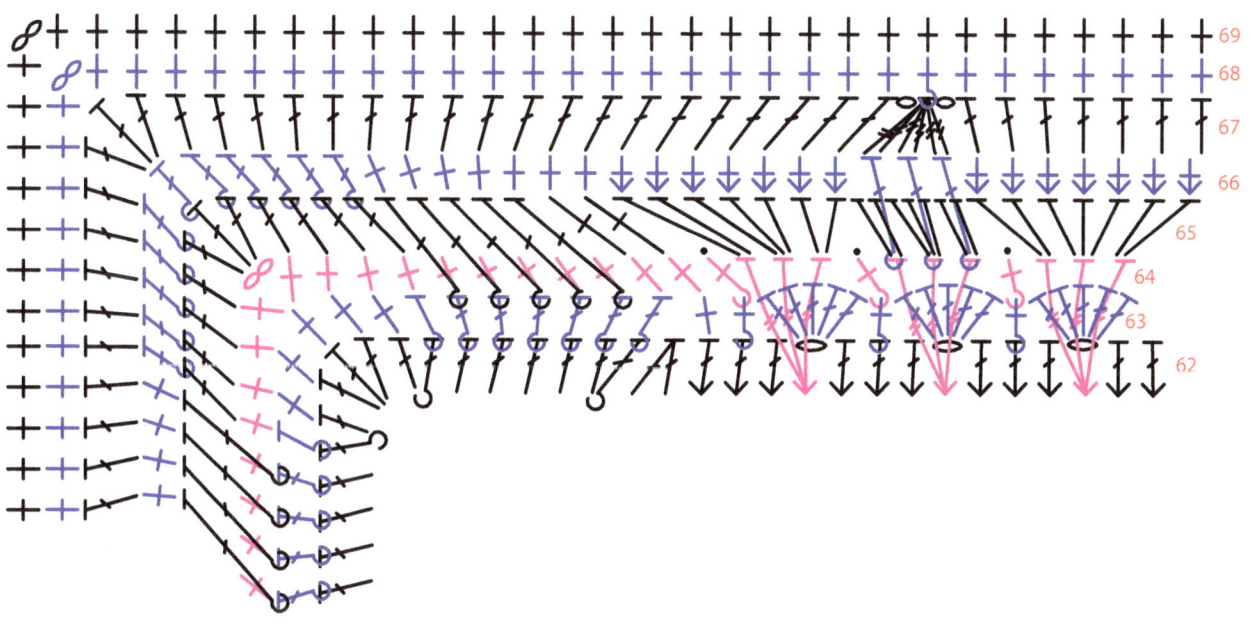

Cabana Days
Right-handed chart

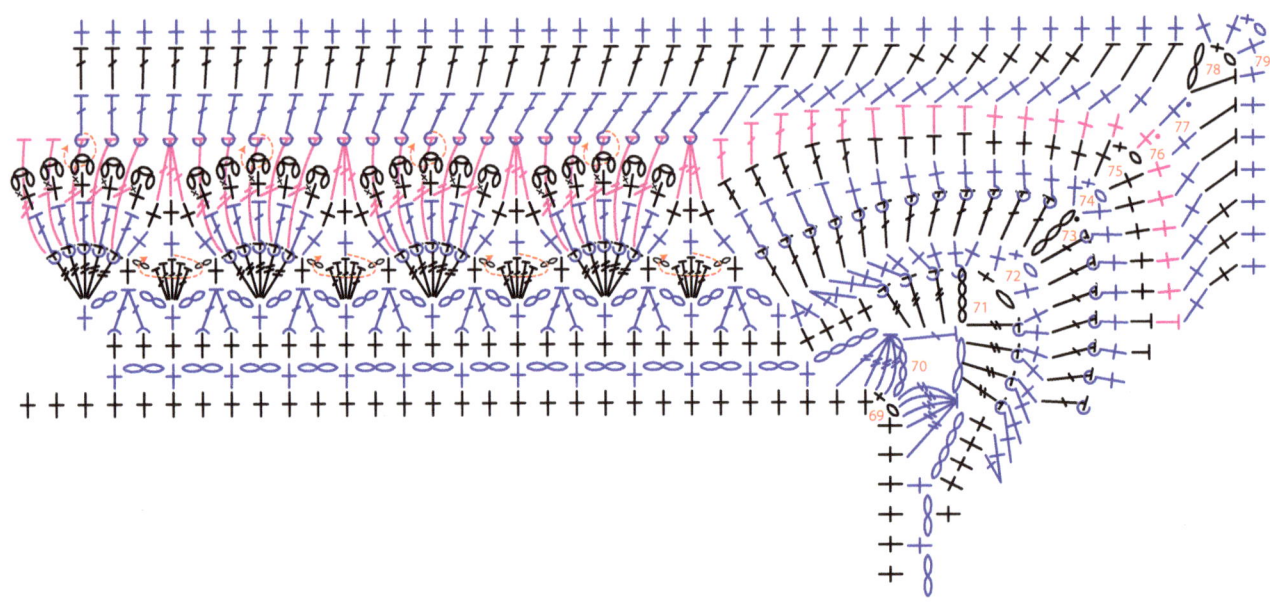

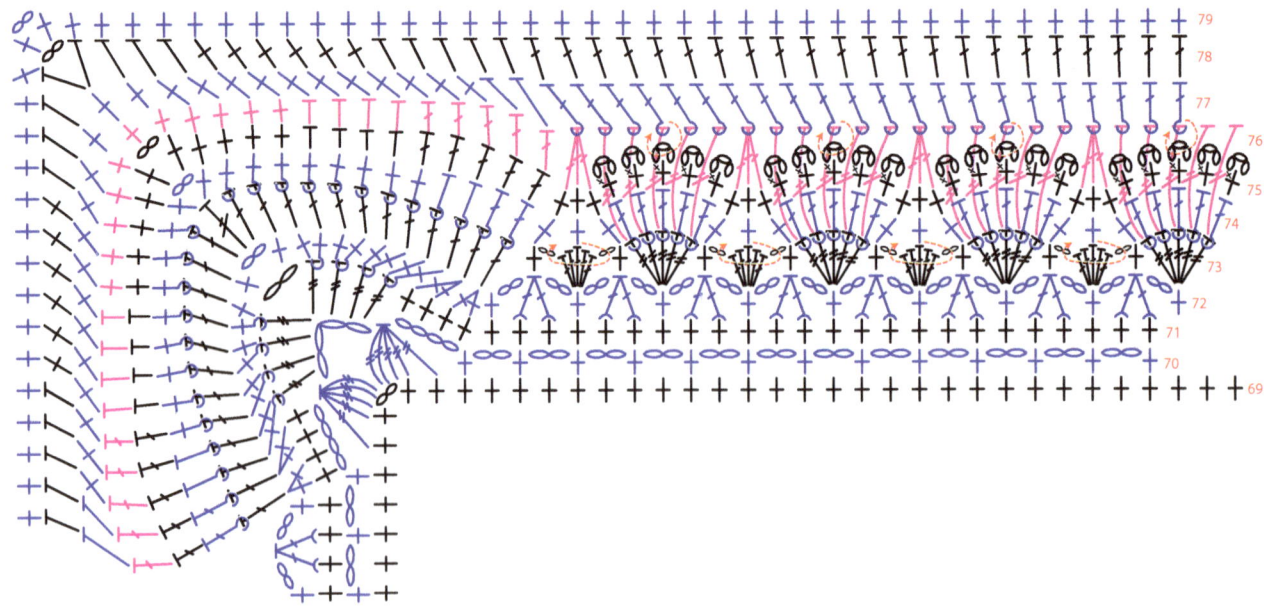

R70: **tr4tog – 2 legs over joining sc & 1 leg each in next 2 sts**
tr5tog – 1 leg each in next 2 sts & 3 legs in 2-ch cnr sp or 3 legs in 2-ch cnr sp & 1 leg each in next 2 sts

ch4 (stch), tr4tog over joining sc & next 2 sts, *ch4, 64x [sc in next st, ch2, skip 1 st], sc in next st, ch4, tr5tog over next 2 sts & 2-ch cnr sp**, ch4, tr5tog over 2-ch cnr sp and next 2 sts*, rep from * to * 2x & * to ** 1x, ch2, join with dc to top of tr4tog.
{67 sts, 2 4-ch sps, 64 2-ch sps on each side; 4 4-ch cnr sps} D

R71: ch4 (stch), 3tr over joining dc, *skip 1 st, 4sc in 4-ch sp, skip 1 st, 63x [sc in 2-ch sp, sc in next st], sc in 2-ch sp, skip 1 st, 4sc in 4-ch sp, skip 1 st**, (4tr, ch2, 4tr) in 4-ch cnr sp*, rep from * to * 2x & * to ** 1x, 4tr in same sp as first sts, ch1, join with sc to 4th ch of stch.
{143 sts on each side; 4 2-ch cnr sps} D

R72: sc over joining sc, *(sc in, fpsc around) next 4 sts, 2x [sc2tog over next 2 sts], 42x [sc in next st, ch2, dc2tog in blo of next 2 sts, ch2], sc in next st, 2x [sc2tog over next 2 sts], (fpsc around, sc in) next 4 sts**, (sc, ch2, sc) in 2-ch cnr sp*, rep from * to * 2x & * to ** 1x, sc in same sp as first st, ch1, join with sc to first st.
{107 sts, 84 2-ch sps on each side; 4 2-ch cnr sps} A

R73: ch3 (stch), dc over joining sc, *dc in next 11 sts, skip (1 st & 2-ch sp), 20x [sc in next st, ch2, skip 2-ch sp, 5dc in next st, ch2, skip 2-ch sp, sc in next st, skip 2-ch sp, 5tr in next st, skip 2-ch sp], sc in next st, ch2, skip 2-ch sp, 5dc in next st, ch2, skip 2-ch sp, sc in next st, skip (2-ch sp & 1 st), dc in next 11 sts**, (dc, htr, dc) in 2-ch cnr sp*, rep from * to * 2x & * to ** 1x, dc in same sp as first sts, join with ss to 3rd ch of stch. **Note: Will be ruffled.**
{269 sts, 42 2-ch sps on each side; 4 3-st cnrs}

R74: sc in same st as ss, *fpsc around next 8 sts, fphdc around next 2 sts, fpdc around next 2 sts, 20x [sc in next st, sc in both 2-ch sps either side of next 5 sts at the same time, sc in next st, fpdc around next 5 sts], sc in next st, sc in both 2-ch sps either side of next 5 sts at the same time, sc in next st, fpdc around next 2 sts, fphdc around next 2 sts, fpsc around next 8 sts**, (sc, ch2, sc) in next st*, rep from * to * 2x & * to ** 1x, sc in same st as first st, ch1, join with sc to first st.
{189 sts on each side; 4 2-ch cnr sps} E

R75: **picot – sc in next st, ch3, sc in sc just made**

sc over joining sc, *sc in next 4 sts, hdc in next 4 sts, dc in next 5 sts, 20x [sc in next 3 sts, picot in next 5 sts], sc in next 3 sts, dc in next 5 sts, hdc in next 4 sts, sc in next 4 sts**, (sc, ch2, sc) in 2-ch cnr sp*, rep from * to * 2x & * to ** 1x, sc in same sp as first sts, ch1, join with sc to first st.
{191 sts on each side; 4 2-ch cnr sps} F

R76: sc over joining sc, *sc in next 5 sts, hdc in next 4 sts, dc in next 5 sts, 20x [dc3tog over next 3 sts, htr in next 5 sts of R73 behind, skip 5 sts], dc3tog over next 3 sts, dc in next 5 sts, hdc in next 4 sts, sc in next 5 sts**, sc in 2-ch cnr sp*, rep from * to * 2x & * to ** 1x, join with ss to first st.
{149 sts on each side; 4 1-st cnrs} Ⓐ

R77: sc in same st as ss, *sc in next 12 sts, hdc in next 2 sts, fpdc around next 3 sts, 19x [bpdc around next st & picot of R75 at the same time, fpdc around next 5 sts], bpdc around next st & picot of R75 at the same time, fpdc around next 3 sts, hdc in next 2 sts, sc in next 12 sts**, sc in next st*, rep from * to * 2x & * to ** 1x, join with ss to first st.
{149 sts on each side; 4 1-st cnrs} Ⓐ

R78: ch2 (stch), *hdc in next 3 sts, sc in next 6 sts, hdc in next 5 sts, dc in next 121 sts, hdc in next 5 sts, sc in next 6 sts, hdc in next 3 sts**, (hdc, ch2, hdc) in next st*, rep from * to * 2x & * to ** 1x, hdc in same st as first st, ch1, join with sc to 2nd ch of stch.
{151 sts on each side; 4 2-ch cnr sps} Ⓐ

R79: sc over joining sc, *skip 1 st, sc in next 150 sts**, (sc, ch2, sc) in 2-ch cnr sp*, rep from * to * 2x & * to ** 1x, sc in same sp as first st,
{152 sts on each side; 4 2-ch cnr sps} Ⓓ

…if taking the Shortcut, ch1, join with sc to first st and continue on to Pebble Beach.

…if taking the Scenic Route, ch2, join with ss to first st. Fasten off. Go to page 40.

Cabana Days

Pebble Beach
Shortcut

Rounds 80 - 88

Find the chart on page 37

Find the Round by Round Help on page 126

R80: ch3 (stch), dc over joining sc, *skip 1 st, dc in next 151 sts**, 3dc in 2-ch cnr sp*, rep from * to * 2x & * to ** 1x, dc in same sp as first sts, join with ss to 3rd ch of stch.
{151 sts on each side; 4 3-st cnrs}

R81: sc in same st as ss, *76x [ch2, skip 1 st, sc in next st], ch2, skip 1 st**, (sc, ch2, sc) in next st*, rep from * to * 2x & * to ** 1x, sc in same st as first st, ch1, join with sc to first st.
{78 sts, 77 2-ch sps on each side; 4 2-ch cnr sps}

R82: dc3tog at start and end of side worked over 1 st and 2-ch sp – 1 leg in the st and 2 legs in the 2-ch sp

ch3 (stch), dc over joining sc, *dc3tog over next st and 2-ch sp, 75x [ch2, skip 1 st, 3dccl in 2-ch sp], ch2, skip 1 st, dc3tog over 2-ch sp and next st**, 3dc in 2-ch cnr sp*, rep from * to * 2x & * to ** 1x, dc in same sp as first sts, join with ss to 3rd ch of stch.
{77 sts, 76 2-ch sps on each side; 4 3-st cnrs}

R83: sc in same st as ss, *sc in next 2 sts, 75x [spike sc over 2-ch sp in skipped st of R81, fpsc around next st], spike sc over 2-ch sp in skipped st of R81, sc in next 2 sts**, (sc, ch2, sc) in next st*, rep from * to * 2x & * to ** 1x, sc in same st as first st, ch1, join with sc to first st.
{157 sts on each side; 4 2-ch cnr sps}

R84: ch3 (stch), dc over joining sc, *dc in next 3 sts, 75x [3dccl in next st, ch1, skip 1 st], 3dccl in next st, dc in next 3 sts**, 3dc in 2-ch cnr sp*, rep from * to * 2x & * to ** 1x, dc in same sp as first sts, join with ss to 3rd ch of stch.
{82 sts, 75 1-ch sps on each side; 4 3-st cnrs}

R85: sc in same st as ss, *sc in next 4 sts, 75x [fpsc around next st, spike sc over 1-ch sp in skipped st of R83], fpsc around next st, sc in next 4 sts**, (sc, ch2, sc) in next st*, rep from * to * 2x & * to ** 1x, sc in same st as first st, ch1, join with sc to first st.
{161 sts on each side; 4 2-ch cnr sps}

Pebble Beach Shortcut
Right-handed charts

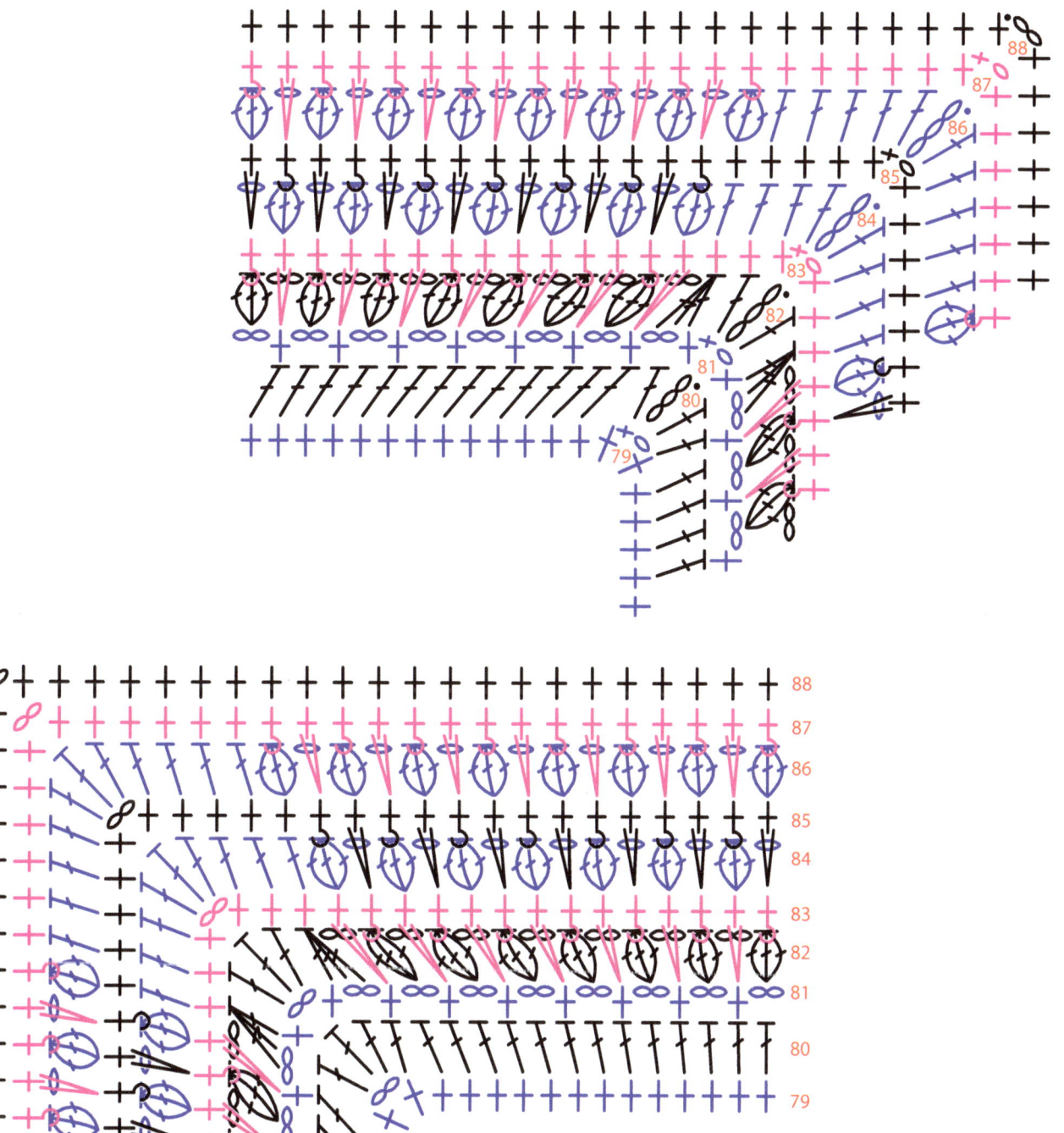

Pebble Beach - Shortcut 37

R86: ch3 (stch), dc over joining sc, *dc in next 4 sts, 76x [3dccl in next st, ch1, skip 1 st], 3dccl in next st, dc in next 4 sts**, 3dc in 2-ch cnr sp*, rep from * to * 2x & * to ** 1x, dc in same sp as first sts, join with ss to 3rd ch of stch.
{85 sts, 76 1-ch sps on each side; 4 3-st cnrs}

R87: sc in same st as ss, *sc in next 5 sts, 76x [fpsc around next st, spike sc over 1-ch sp in skipped st of R85], fpsc around next st, sc in next 5 sts**, (sc, ch2, sc) in next st*, rep from * to * 2x & * to ** 1x, sc in same st as first st, ch1, join with sc to first st.
{165 sts on each side; 4 2-ch cnr sps}

R88: sc over joining sc, *sc in next 165 sts**, (sc, ch2, sc) in 2-ch cnr sp*, rep from * to * 2x & * to ** 1x, sc in same sp as first st, ch2, join with ss to first st. Fasten off.
{167 sts on each side; 4 2-ch cnr sps}

Take a rest now you have arrived at your destination!

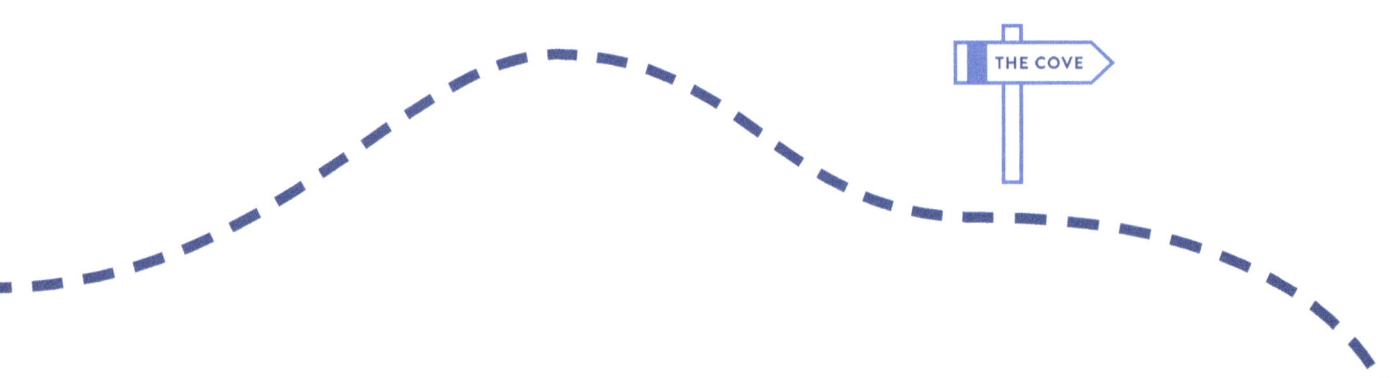

Scenic Route
Directions

Taking the longer path around The Cove?

The Scenic Route has some marvels to show you as you take the longer path. There are four different small squares to make.

Make 8 Sunset Shells, Fans and Ripples squares.

Make 4 Wicker squares.

Joining method:

Hold squares right sides together, attach joining yarn with a standing single crochet to both 2-chain corner spaces of each square at the same time.

Work a single crochet stitch into both loops of both squares all the way along, end with a stitch in both 2-chain corner spaces. Fasten off.

When the stitch counts differ, use the same stitch twice on the smaller stitch count square while using a new stitch on the larger stitch count square as many times as necessary to account for the difference.

Small Squares	Stitch Count
Sunset Shells	29
Ripples	25
Fans	30
Wicker	25

Join 2 strips of 6 squares as shown in blue. Join 2 strips of 8 squares as shown in grey.

Attach the 6-square strips to opposite sides of the centre panel. Along the side, 26 times, use the same stitch on the centre panel twice while always using a new stitch, or space on the strip. Ignore the joins on the strip.

Then attach the 8-square strips to the unused sides of the centre panel.

Now you are ready to move on to the Pebble Beach Border.

W	S	R	F	S	R	F	W
F							S
R							R
S							F
F							S
R							R
S							F
W	F	R	S	F	R	S	W

Scenic Route

Sunset Shells
Small Pattern

Find the chart on page 43

Find the Round by Round Help on page 132

Begin with mc.

R1: ch3 (stch), 2dc around stch, *dc, 2dc around dc just made*, rep from * to * 6x, join with ss to 3rd ch of stch.
{24 sts}

R2: sc in same st as ss, sc in next 23 sts, join with ss to first st.
{24 sts}

R3: ch3 (stch), *2dc in next st**, dc in next st*, rep from * to * 10x & * to ** 1x, join with ss to 3rd ch of stch.
{36 sts}

R4: sc in same st as ss, *ch2, fpss around next 2 sts, ch2**, sc in next st*, rep from * to * 10x & * to ** 1x, join with ss to first st.
{36 sts, 24 2-ch sps}

R5: **Note: "dc4tog over 2 sts" – begin 2 sts in each st**

sc in same st as ss, *ch1, dc4tog over next 2 sts of R3, ch1, skip (2-ch sp, 2 sts & 2-ch sp)**, sc in next st*, rep from * to * 10x & * to ** 1x, join with ss to first st.
{24 sts, 24 1-ch sps}

R6: sc in same st as ss, *2sc in 1-ch sp, skip 1 st, 2sc in 1-ch sp**, sc in next st*, rep from * to * 10x & * to ** 1x, join with ss to first st.
{60 sts}

R7: ch4 (stch), tr in same st as ss, *htr in next 2 sts, dc in next 2 sts, hdc in next 2 sts, sc in next 2 sts, hdc in next 2 sts, dc in next 2 sts, htr in next 2 sts**, 3tr in next st*, rep from * to * 2x & * to ** 1x, tr in same st as first sts, join with ss to 4th ch of stch.
{14 sts on each side; 4 3-st cnrs}

42   Sunset Shells

R8: sc in same st as ss, *sc in next 16 sts**, (sc, ch2, sc) in next st*, rep from * to * 2x & * to ** 1x, sc in same st as first st, ch1, join with sc to first st.
{18 sts on each side; 4 2-ch cnr sps}

R9: sc over joining sc, *4x [ch3, skip 3 sts, sc in next st], ch3, skip 2 sts**, (sc, ch2, sc) in 2-ch cnr sp*, rep from * to * 2x & * to ** 1x, sc in same sp as first st, ch1, join with sc to first st.
{6 sts, 5 3-ch sps on each side; 4 2-ch cnr sps}

R10: sc over joining sc, *2x [skip 1 st, 5dc in 3-ch sp, skip 1 st, sc in 3-ch sp], skip 1 st, 5dc in 3-ch sp, skip 1 st**, (sc, ch2, sc) in 2-ch cnr sp*, rep from * to * 2x & * to ** 1x, sc in same sp as first st, ch1, join with sc to first st.
{19 sts on each side; 4 2-ch cnr sps}

R11: ch3 (stch), 2dc over joining sc, *dc in next st, sc in lbv of next 3 sts, skip 2 sts, 5dc in next st, skip 2 sts, sc in lbv of next st, skip 2 sts, 5dc in next st, skip 2 sts, sc in lbv of next 3 sts, dc in next st**, 5dc in 2-ch cnr sp*, rep from * to * 2x & * to ** 1x, 2dc in same sp as first sts, join with ss to 3rd ch of stch.
{19 sts on each side; 4 5-st cnrs}

R12: sc in same st as ss, *sc in next 3 sts, hdc in next 3 sts, sc in lbv of next 3 sts, skip 2 sts, 5dc in next st, skip 2 sts, sc in lbv of next 3 sts, hdc in next 3 sts, sc in next 3 sts**, (sc, ch2, sc) in next st*, rep from * to * 2x & * to ** 1x, sc in same st as first st, ch1, join with sc to first st.
{25 sts on each side; 4 2-ch cnr sps} C

R13: ch3 (stch), dc over joining sc, *dc in next 7 sts, hdc in next 3 sts, sc in lbv of next 5 sts, hdc in next 3 sts, dc in next 7 sts**, 3dc in 2-ch cnr sp*, rep from * to * 2x & * to ** 1x, dc in same sp as first sts, join with ss to 3rd ch of stch.
{25 sts on each side; 4 3-st cnrs} A

R14: sc in same st as ss, *sc in blo of next 27 sts**, (sc, ch2, sc) in next st *, rep from * to * 2x & * to ** 1x, sc in same st as first st, ch2, join with ss to first st. Fasten off.
{29 sts on each side; 4 2-ch cnr sps} D

Sunset Shells

Sunset Shells

Ripples
Small Pattern

Find the chart on page 47

Find the Round by Round Help on page 136

Begin with mc.

R1: ch3 (stch), 15dc, join with ss to 3rd ch of stch. {16 sts}

R2: ch3 (stch), *2dc in next st, 2dc in blo of next st, 2dc in next st**, dc in next st*, rep from * to * 2x & * to ** 1x, join with ss to 3rd ch of stch. {28 sts}

R3: ch3 (stch), *bpdc around next 2 sts, dc in blo of next 2 sts, bpdc around next 2 sts**, 2dc in next st*, rep from * to * 2x & * to ** 1x, dc in same st as first st, join with ss to 3rd ch of stch. {32 sts}

R4: ch3 (stch), dc in same st as ss, *2dc in next st, dc in next st, 2dc in blo of next st, dc in blo of next st, 2dc in next st, dc in next st**, 2dc in next 2 sts*, rep from * to * 2x & * to ** 1x, 2dc in next st, join with ss to 3rd ch of stch. {52 sts}

R5: ch3 (stch), *bpdc around next 4 sts, dc in blo of next 3 sts, bpdc around next 4 sts**, dc in next 2 sts*, rep from * to * 2x & * to ** 1x, dc in next st, join with ss to 3rd ch of stch. {52 sts}

R6: ch3 (stch), dc in next 4 sts, *2dc in blo of next st, dc in blo of next st, 2dc in blo of next st**, dc in next 10 sts*, rep from * to * 2x & * to ** 1x, dc in next 5 sts, join with ss to 3rd ch of stch. {60 sts}

R7: ch3 (stch), *bpdc around next 4 sts, dc in blo of next 5 sts, bpdc around next 4 sts**, dc in next 2 sts*, rep from * to * 2x & * to ** 1x, dc in next st, join with ss to 3rd ch of stch. {60 sts}

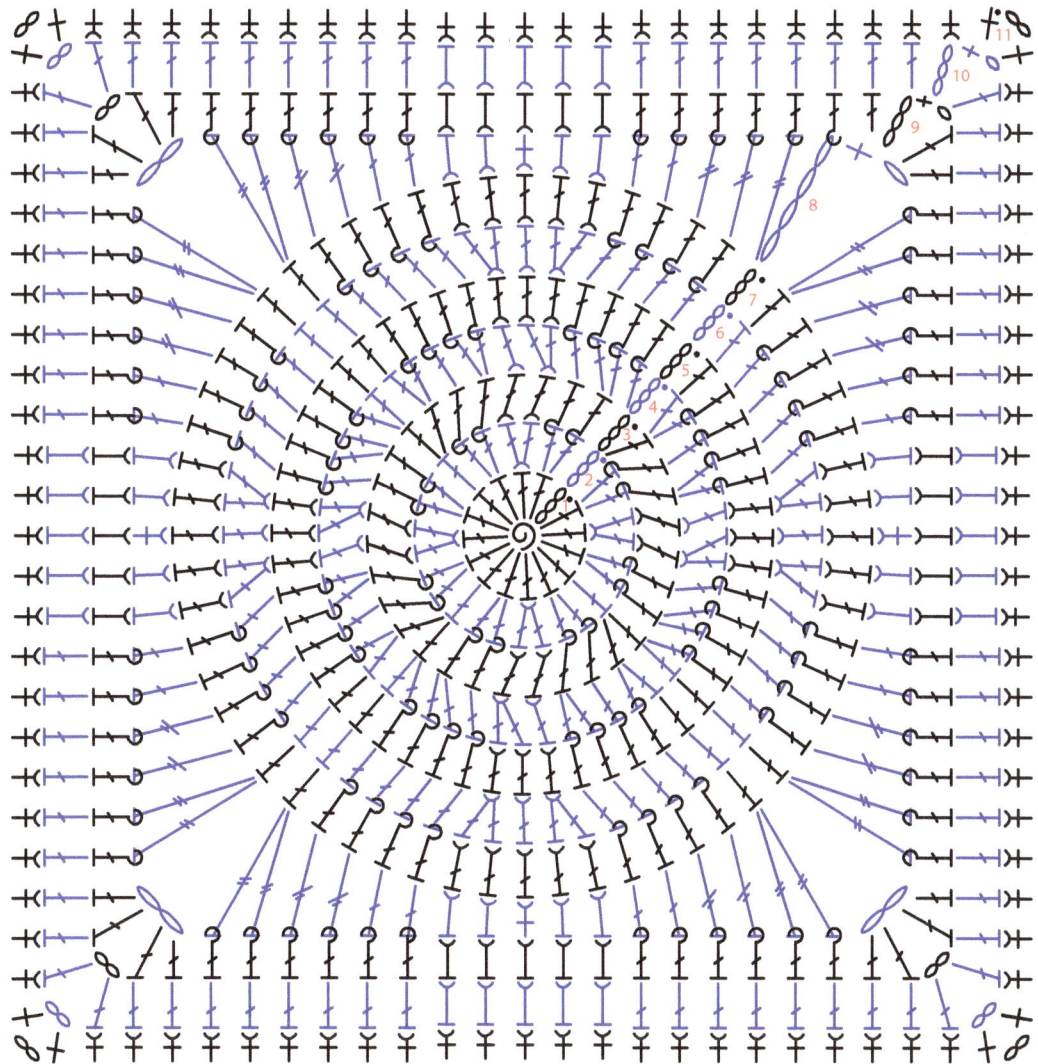

R8: ch4 (stch), tr in same st as ss, *htr in next 2 sts, dc in next 2 sts, hdc in blo of next 2 sts, sc in blo of next st, hdc in blo of next 2 sts, dc in next 2 sts, htr in next 2 sts, 2tr in next st**, ch2, 2tr in next st*, rep from * to * 2x & * to ** 1x, ch1, join with sc to 4th ch of stch.
{17 sts on each side; 4 2-ch cnr sps} **F**

R9: ch3 (stch), dc over joining sc, *bpdc around next 6 sts, hdc in blo of next 5 sts, bpdc around next 6 sts**, (2dc, ch2, 2dc) in 2-ch cnr sp*, rep from * to * 2x & * to ** 1x, 2dc in same sp as first sts, ch1, join with sc to 3rd ch of stch.
{21 sts on each side; 4 2-ch cnr sps} **C**

R10: ch3 (stch), *dc in next 8 sts, hdc in blo of next 5 sts, dc in next 8 sts**, (dc, ch2, dc) in 2-ch cnr sp*, rep from * to * 2x & * to ** 1x, dc in same sp as first st, ch1, join with sc to 3rd ch of stch.
{23 sts on each side; 4 2-ch cnr sps} **A**

R11: sc over joining sc, *sc in blo of next 23 sts**, (sc, ch2, sc) in 2-ch cnr sp*, rep from * to * 2x & * to ** 1x, sc in same sp as first st, ch2, join with ss to first st. Fasten off.
{25 sts on each side; 4 2-ch cnr sps} **D**

Ripples

Fans
Small Pattern

Find the chart on page 49

Find the Round by Round Help on page 141

Begin with mc.

R1: ch3 (stch), *ch2, dc4tog, ch2**, dc*, rep from * to * 2x & * to ** 1x, join with ss to 3rd ch of stch.
{8 sts, 8 2-ch sps} E

R2: sc in same st as ss, *2sc in 2-ch sp, fpsc around next st, 2sc in 2-ch sp**, sc in next st*, rep from * to * 2x & * to ** 1x, join with ss to first st.
{24 sts} D

R3: ch3 (stch), dc in same st as ss, *hdc in next st, sc in next 3 sts, hdc in next st**, 3dc in next st*, rep from * to * 2x & * to ** 1x, dc in same st as first sts, join with ss to 3rd ch of stch.
{5 sts on each side; 4 3-st cnrs} A

R4: sc in same st as ss, *sc in next 7 sts**, (sc, ch2, sc) in next st*, rep from * to * 2x & * to ** 1x, sc in same st as first st, ch1, join with sc to first st.
{9 sts on each side; 4 2-ch cnr sps} A

R5: ch3 (stch), *ch2, dc4tog over next 4 sts, ch2, sc in next st, ch2, dc4tog over next 4 sts, ch2**, (dc, ch2, dc) in 2-ch cnr sp*, rep from * to * 2x & * to ** 1x, dc in same sp as first st, ch1, join with sc to 3rd ch of stch.
{5 sts, 4 2-ch sps on each side; 4 2-ch cnr sps} C

R6: sc over joining sc, *sc in next st, 2sc in 2-ch sp, sc in next st, skip 2-ch sp, 4dc in next st, skip 2-ch sp, sc in next st, 2sc in 2-ch sp, sc in next st**, (sc, ch2, sc) in 2-ch cnr sp*, rep from * to * 2x & * to ** 1x, sc in same sp as first st, ch1, join with sc to first st.
{14 sts on each side; 4 2-ch cnr sps} D

R7: sc over joining sc, *sc in next 4 sts, fpdc around R5 cl below, ch1, bpdc around next R5 st, ch1, fpdc around R5 cl below, skip 6 sts, sc in next 4 sts**, (sc, ch2, sc) in 2-ch cnr sp*, rep from * to * 2x & * to ** 1x, sc in same sp as first st, ch1, join with sc to first st.
{13 sts, 2 1-ch sps on each side; 4 2-ch cnr sps} D

R8: ch3 (stch), *dc in next 6 sts, dc in 1-ch sp, dc in next st, dc in 1-ch sp, dc in next 6 sts**, (dc, ch2, dc) in 2-ch cnr sp*, rep from * to * 2x & * to ** 1x, dc in same sp as first st, ch1, join with sc to 3rd ch of stch.
{17 sts on each side; 4 2-ch cnr sps}

R9: ch3 (stch), 2dc over joining sc, *ch2, 2x [dc5tog over next 5 sts, ch3, sc in next st, ch3], dc5tog over next 5 sts, ch2**, 5dc in 2-ch cnr sp*, rep from * to * 2x & * to ** 1x, 2dc in same sp as first sts, join with ss to 3rd ch of stch.
{5 sts, 4 3-ch sps, 2 2-ch sps on each side; 4 5-st cnrs}

R10: sc in same st as ss, *sc in next 2 sts, 2sc in 2-ch sp, 2x [sc in next st, skip 3-ch sp, 5dc in next st, skip 3-ch sp], sc in next st, 2sc in 2-ch sp, sc in next 2 sts**, (sc, ch2, sc) in next st*, rep from * to * 2x & * to ** 1x, sc in same st as first st, ch1, join with sc to first st.
{23 sts on each side; 4 2-ch cnr sps}

Fans

49

R11: sc over joining sc, *sc in next 5 sts, 2x [fpdc around R9 cl below, ch1, bpdc around next R9 st, ch1], fpdc around R9 cl below, skip 13 sts, sc in next 5 sts**, (sc, ch2, sc) in 2-ch cnr sp*, rep from * to * 2x & * to ** 1x, sc in same sp as first st, ch1, join with sc to first st.
{17 sts, 4 1-ch sps on each side; 4 2-ch cnr sps} Ⓓ

R12: ch3 (stch), *dc in next 7 sts, 3x [dc in 1-ch sp, 2dc in next st], dc in 1-ch sp, dc in next 7 sts**, (dc, ch2, dc) in 2-ch cnr sp*, rep from * to * 2x & * to ** 1x, dc in same sp as first st, ch1, join with sc to 3rd ch of stch.
{26 sts on each side; 4 2-ch cnr sps} Ⓐ

R13: sc over joining sc, *sc in blo of next 26 sts**, (sc, ch2, sc) in 2-ch cnr sp*, rep from * to * 2x & * to ** 1x, sc in same sp as first st, ch1, join with sc to first st.
{28 sts on each side; 4 2-ch cnr sps} Ⓐ

R14: sc over joining sc, *sc in blo of next 28 sts**, (sc, ch2, sc) in 2-ch cnr sp*, rep from * to * 2x & * to ** 1x, sc in same sp as first st, ch2, join with ss to first st. Fasten off.
{30 sts on each side; 4 2-ch cnr sps} Ⓓ

Fans

Wicker
Small Pattern

Find the chart on page 53

Find the Round by Round Help on page 146

Begin with mc.

R1: ch1, 12sc, join with ss to first st.
{12 sts} B

R2: ch3 (stch), *2dc in next st**, dc in next st*, rep from * to * 4x & * to ** 1x, join with ss to 3rd ch of stch.
{18 sts} E

R3: sc in same st as ss, *2sc in next st**, sc in next 2 sts*, rep from * to * 4x & * to ** 1x, sc in next st, join with ss to first st.
{24 sts} F

R4: ch4 (stch), (htr, dc) in same st as ss, *dc in next st, hdc in next st, sc in next st, hdc in next st, dc in next st**, (dc, htr, tr, htr, dc) in next st*, rep from * to * 2x & * to ** 1x, (dc, htr) in same st as first sts, join with ss to 4th ch of stch.
{5 sts along each side; 4 5-st cnrs} A

R5: sc in same st as ss, *sc in next 9 sts**, (sc, ch2, sc) in next st*, rep from * to * 2x & * to ** 1x, sc in same st as first st, ch1, join with sc to first st.
{11 sts on each side; 4 2-ch cnr sps} D

R6: ch3 (stch), dc over joining sc, *dc in next 11 sts**, 3dc in 2-ch cnr sp*, rep from * to * 2x & * to ** 1x, dc in same sp as first sts, join with ss to 3rd ch of stch.
{11 sts on each side; 4 3-st cnrs} C

R7: ch3 (stch), dc in same st as ss, *6x [dc in next st, fpdc around next st], dc in next st**, 3dc in next st*, rep from * to * 2x & * to ** 1x, dc in same st as first sts, join with ss to 3rd ch of stch.
{13 sts on each side; 4 3-st cnrs} B

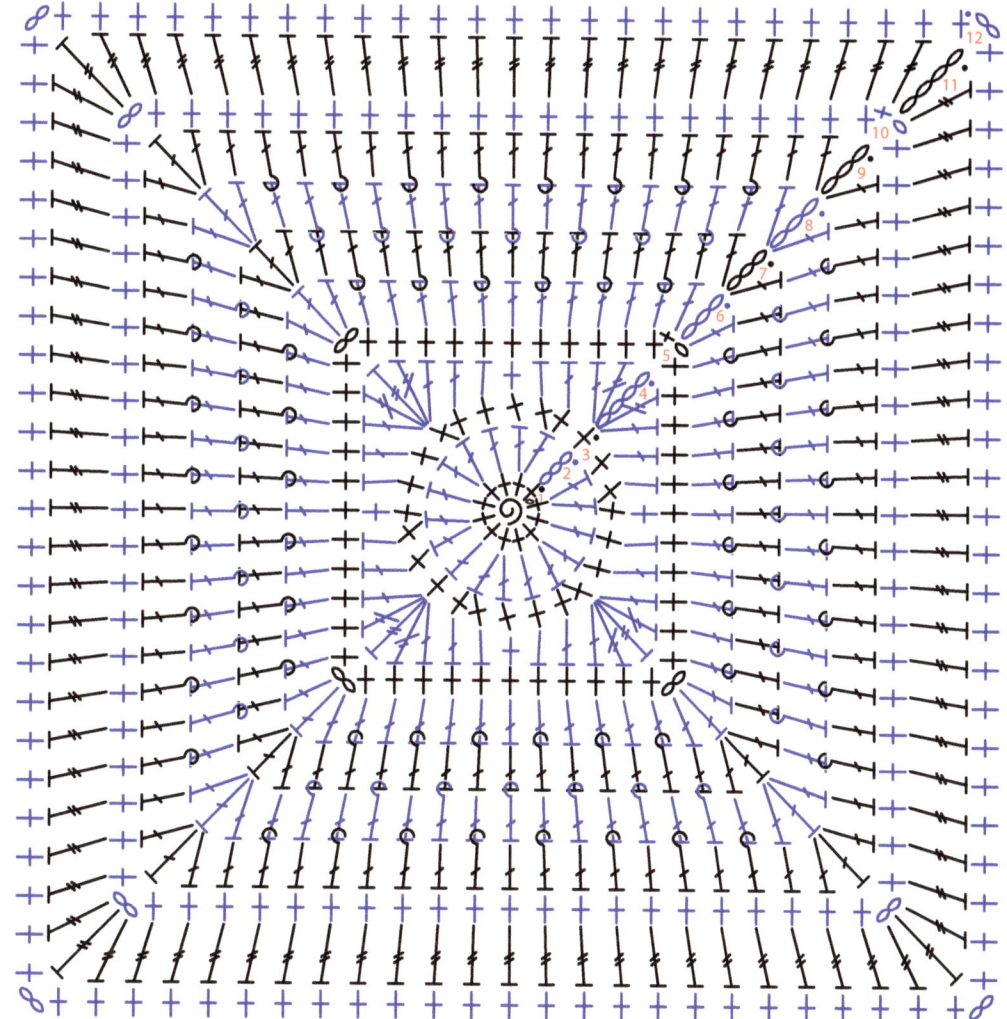

R8: ch3 (stch), dc in same st as ss, *7x [dc in next st, fpdc around next st], dc in next st**, 3dc in next st*, rep from * to * 2x & * to ** 1x, dc in same st as first sts, join with ss to 3rd ch of stch.
{15 sts on each side; 4 3-st cnrs} E

R9: ch3 (stch), dc in same st as ss, *8x [dc in next st, fpdc around next st], dc in next st**, 3dc in next st*, rep from * to * 2x & * to ** 1x, dc in same st as first sts, join with ss to 3rd ch of stch.
{17 sts on each side; 4 3-st cnrs} F

R10: sc in same st as ss, *sc in next 19 sts**, (sc, ch2, sc) in next st*, rep from * to * 2x & * to ** 1x, sc in same st as first st, ch1, join with sc to first st.
{21 sts on each side; 4 2-ch cnr sps} D

R11: ch4 (stch), tr over joining sc, *tr in next 21 sts**, 3tr in 2-ch cnr sp*, rep from * to * 2x & * to ** 1x, tr in same sp as first sts, join with ss to 4th ch of stch.
{21 sts on each side; 4 3-st cnrs} A

R12: sc in same st as ss, *sc in next 23 sts**, (sc, ch2, sc) in next st*, rep from * to * 2x & * to ** 1x, sc in same st as first st, ch2, join with ss to first st. Fasten off.
{25 sts on each side; 4 2-ch cnr sps} D

Pebble Beach
Scenic Route
Rounds 80 - 89

Find the chart on page 55

Find the Round by Round Help on page 126

R80: Attach with stdg sc to any 2-ch cnr sp, *sc in each st, ch sp and join along side**, (sc, ch2, sc) in 2-ch cnr sp*, rep from * to * 2x &* to ** 1x, sc in same sp as first st, ch1, join with sc to first st.
{241 sts on each side, 4 2-ch cnr sps} D

R81: ch3 (stch), dc over joining sc, *dc in next 241 sts**, 3dc in 2-ch cnr sp*, rep from * to * 2x & * to ** 1x, dc in same sp as first sts, join with ss to 3rd ch of stch.
{241 sts on each side; 4 3-st cnrs} A

R82: sc in same st as ss, *121x [ch2, skip 1 st, sc in next st], ch2, skip 1 st**, (sc, ch2, sc) in next st*, rep from * to * 2x &* to ** 1x, sc in same st as first st, ch1, join with sc to first st.
{123 sts, 122 2-ch sps on each side; 4 2-ch cnr sps} A

R83: dc3tog at start and end of side worked over 1 st and 2-ch sp – 1 leg in the st and 2 legs in the 2-ch sp

ch3 (stch), dc over joining sc, *dc3tog over next st and 2-ch sp, 120x [ch2, skip 1 st, 3dccl in 2-ch sp], ch2, skip 1 st, dc3tog over 2-ch sp and next st**, 3dc in 2-ch cnr sp*, rep from * to * 2x & * to ** 1x, dc in same sp as first sts, join with ss to 3rd ch of stch.
{122 sts, 121 2-ch sps on each side; 4 3-st cnrs} B

R84: sc in same st as ss, *sc in next 2 sts, 120x [spike sc over 2-ch sp in skipped st of R82, fpsc around next st], spike sc over 2-ch sp in skipped st of R82, sc in next 2 sts**, (sc, ch2, sc) in next st*, rep from * to * 2x &* to ** 1x, sc in same st as first st, ch1, join with sc to first st.
{247 sts on each side; 4 2-ch cnr sps} A

R85: ch3 (stch), dc over joining sc, *dc in next 3 sts, 120x [3dccl in next st, ch1, skip 1 st], 3dccl in next st, dc in next 3 sts**, 3dc in 2-ch cnr sp*, rep from * to * 2x & * to ** 1x, dc in same sp as first sts, join with ss to 3rd ch of stch.
{127 sts, 120 1-ch sps on each side; 4 3-st cnrs} E

Pebble Beach Scenic Route
Right-handed charts

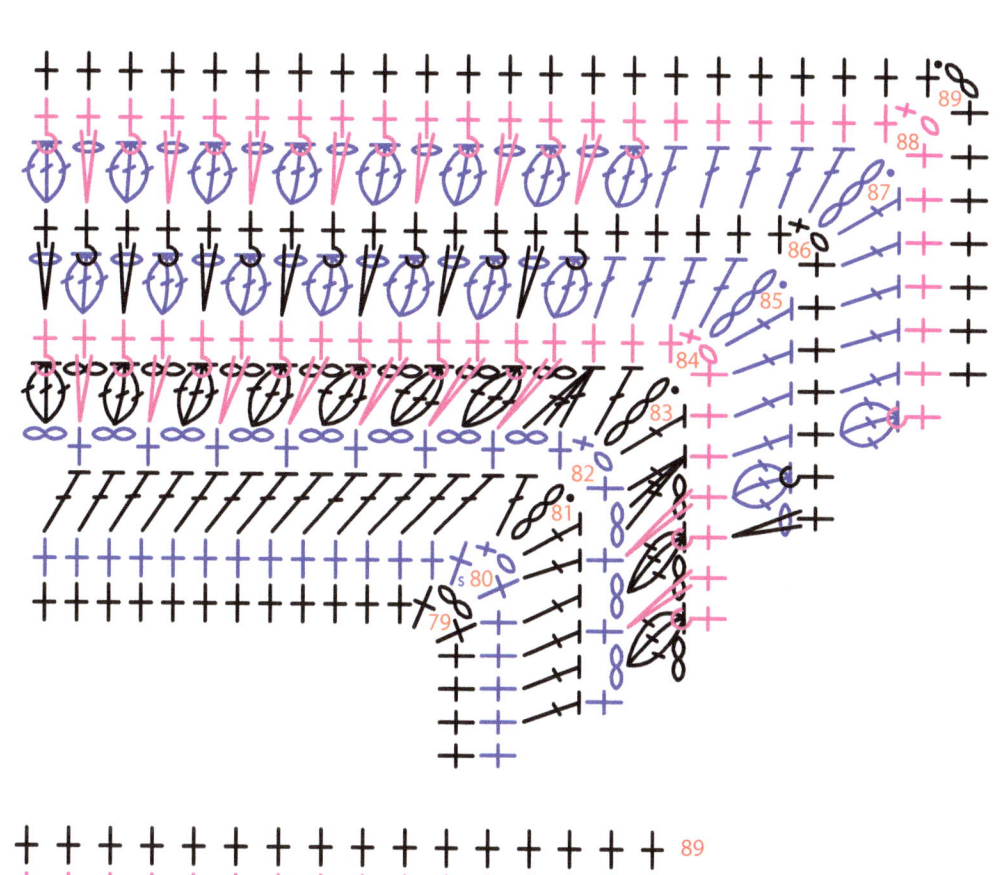

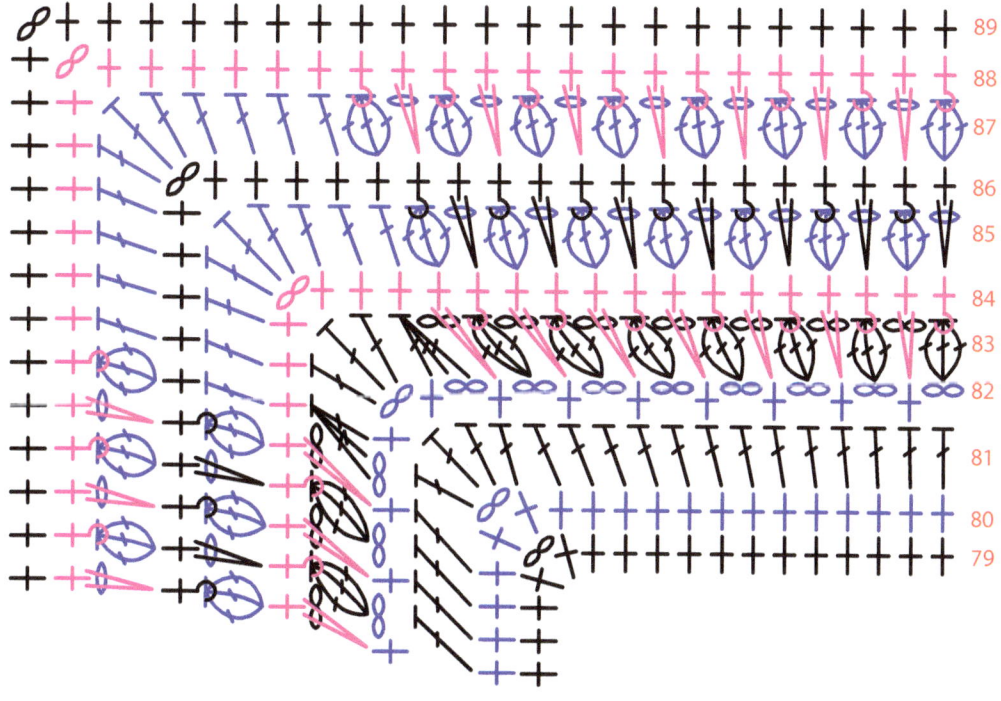

Pebble Beach - Scenic Route

R86: sc in same st as ss, *sc in next 4 sts, 120x [fpsc around next st, spike sc over 1-ch sp in skipped st of R84], fpsc around next st, sc in next 4 sts**, (sc, ch2, sc) in next st*, rep from * to * 2x & * to ** 1x, sc in same st as first st, ch1, join with sc to first st.
{251 sts on each side; 4 2-ch cnr sps} Ⓐ

R87: ch3 (stch), dc over joining sc, *dc in next 4 sts, 121x [3dccl in next st, ch1, skip 1 st], 3dccl in next st, dc in next 4 sts**, 3dc in 2-ch cnr sp*, rep from * to * 2x & * to ** 1x, dc in same sp as first sts, join with ss to 3rd ch of stch.
{130 sts, 121 1-ch sps on each side; 4 3-st cnrs} Ⓕ

R88: sc in same st as ss, *sc in next 5 sts, 121x [fpsc around next st, spike sc over 1-ch sp in skipped st of R86], fpsc around next st, sc in next 5 sts**, (sc, ch2, sc) in next st*, rep from * to * 2x & * to ** 1x, sc in same st as first st, ch1, join with sc to first st.
{255 sts on each side; 4 2-ch cnr sps} Ⓐ

R89: sc over joining sc, *sc in next 255 sts**, (sc, ch2, sc) in 2-ch cnr sp*, rep from * to * 2x & * to ** 1x, sc in same sp as first st, ch2, join with ss to first st. Fasten off.
{257 sts on each side; 4 2-ch cnr sps} Ⓓ

Pebble Beach - Scenic Route

Pebble Beach - Scenic Route

Guide Book

This Guide book will keep you on the right path and show you interesting things as you pass the sights of The Cove.

At the start of each section, there is a QR code to scan that will take you to the video (or mirrored video) for that section. The description in YouTube has timings for every five rounds or so to help you find the bit you need.

The videos show all the important things, but not the "same stitch in every stitch" rounds.

Try this!

While I state to begin with a number of chains at the start of some rounds, I prefer to work a false stitch instead. You will see me making this in the videos. It is optional. Working the number of chains is fine if you prefer.

Try this!

The Lighthouses light up things you can apply to your crochet beyond The Cove.

Signposts point out important facts specific to the area you are visiting.

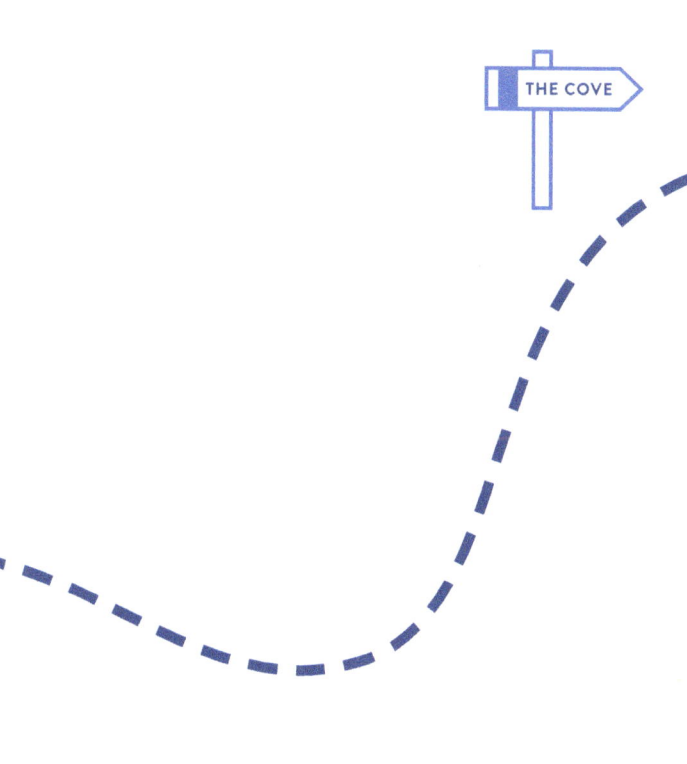

Now it's time to put on your hiking boots, hoist your backpack and start on our relaxing trek around The Cove.

Coastal Sunrise
Round by round help

 Coastal Sunrise video

 Coastal Sunrise mirrored video

Watch the sun rise over the ocean from the clifftops above The Cove.

R1

We'll be starting off our adventures in The Cove with an interesting way to make stitches. They are all regular stitches, but where you place the second and third stitches may be new to you. Only 8 of the 24 stitches of Round 1 are worked into the magic circle.

 **Try this!**

To make it easy to see where to join to at the end of the round, pop a stitch marker in the third chain of your starting chain or false stitch.

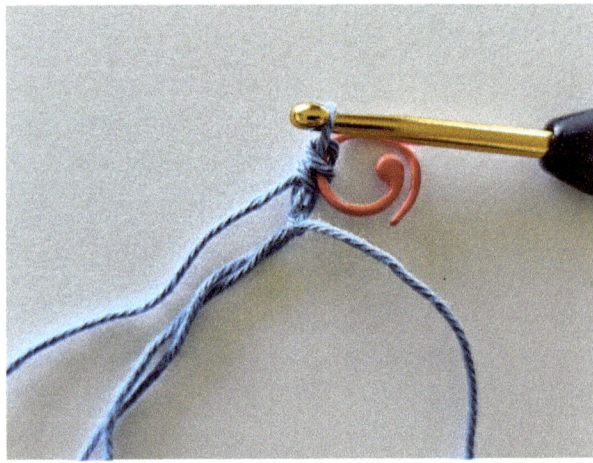

After starting with chain 3 or the false stitch, the next 2 stitches are worked around that starting chain or false stitch.

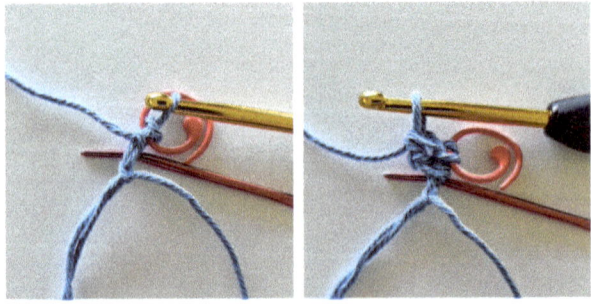

The red needle shows where to work the first and second stitch, around the stitch just made.

Then, your next stitch is worked into the magic circle before it has 2 stitches worked around it. There will be 8 of these 3-stitch combinations in the round.

Two of eight stitch shapes made

R1

R2

Round 2 is super easy! Starting with a small stitch in the same stitch as your slip stitch join of Round 1, work a small stitch in every stitch.

 **Try this!**

When a round begins with a small stitch, popping a stitch marker in it as soon as you make it will make reading the stitches at the end of the round easier.

R2

Coastal Sunrise Help

R3

An easy round alternating between a single stitch in the 1 stitch and 2 stitches in the next stitch.

Work 1 stitch where the red needle is and 2 where the silver is.

R3

R4

After working your stitch in the same stitch as the slip stitch and chaining 2, you work a front post slip stitch around each of the next 2 stitches. The red needle shows where to work the first front post slip stitch.

Front post slip stitches are worked around the two stitches made in one stitch (silver needles) while the single stitch made in one stitch has a small stitch worked into it (red needle). You need to chain 2 before and after each 2 front post slip stitches.

> **THIS WAY**
>
> The front post slip stitches are included in the stitch count. As always, the joining slip stitch is not.

R4

R5

A fun round! After beginning with a small stitch in the same stitch that the slip stitch was worked into, you will chain 1. Then you crochet a 4-together stitch, but 2 legs of the stitch are worked into each of the 2 stitches of Round 3, the ones we slip stitched around in Round 4.

Work 2 legs in each of these stitches

> **THIS WAY**
>
> It may help to pull the chains down to expose the stitches to work into.

Then you chain 1 and skip the 2-chain space, the 2 front post slip stitches and the next 2-chain space before working a small stitch in the next stitch.

R5

Coastal Sunrise Help

R6

Nice and easy! Starting with a small stitch in the same stitch as slip stitch, the 2-chain spaces each have 2 small stitches worked into them, the small stitches have 1 stitch worked into them and the together stitches are skipped.

Skip together stitch

R6

> **THIS WAY**
>
> Finish here for a cute coaster. For a seamless edge, begin with chain 1 instead of the small stitch in same stitch as slip stitch and end with an invisible join to the first small stitch. This is shown in the video.

The silver needles show where to work 2 stitches into each 1-chain space and the red needle shows where to work the next stitch in stitch.

There are 5 stitches in the repeat, giving you 60 stitches at the end of this round.

Reef Ripples
Round by round help

 Reef Ripples video

 Reef Ripples mirrored video

Pause on the shore to watch the sea rippling in from the reef.

R7

An easy part of the track with a regular stitch in every stitch. You won't stumble.

R7

R8

No stitches of this round are worked into stitches! They are all worked between stitches.

The instructions say to work a stitch between the last and next stitches. At the start, the last stitch is the stitch you joined into with a slip stitch and the next stitch is the next unworked stitch. You work your first stitch between those stitches.

The red needle shows where to work the first stitch.

From then on, you work a stitch between all stitches of the last round. You will still have 60 stitches.

R8

R9

Lots of stitches in this round! After the usual small stitch at the start, skip 2 stitches then work all of the stitches in the brackets into the next stitch. That is; 2 stitches, chain 1, 5 stitches, chain 1 and 2 more stitches, all in the one stitch.

Skip 2 stitches before working a single small stitch in the next stitch. Be careful reading your stitches here, as working all those stitches into one could hide the first stitch to skip.

The red needle shows where to work the next small stitch after skipping 2 stitches.

R9

 **THIS WAY**

Make sure you have ten shell shapes before moving on to Round 10.

Reef Ripples Help

R10

The start of this round is chain 3 plus a 4-stitch cluster, which together represent a 5-stitch cluster.

At the end of the round, join to the top of the 4-stitch cluster to make the chain 3 disappear.

After chaining 1, work a stitch into the next 2 stitches. Now comes the fun bit. Insert your hook in both 1-chain spaces either side of the 5 stitches and gather them with 1 small stitch.

Join to top of 4-st cluster

 **Try this!**

You can begin to work a false stitch at the beginning and make a 5-stitch cluster from the very start.

Then, work a stitch in the next 2 stitches before chaining 1 and making your next 5-stitch cluster in the next stitch.

> **THIS WAY**
>
> The 5-stitch clusters will always be worked into the dip between the shells. There are 5 stitches between the 1-chain spaces.

5 stitches with a chain either side between the needles

R10

R11

Another easy section of the path; a small stitch in every stitch and chain space.

R11

R12

Now in this round, all stitches are worked around the Round 10 stitches. The first stitch is a front post stitch around the 5-stitch cluster below.

> **THIS WAY**
>
> Pop a stitch marker in that first front post stitch as soon as you make it to make it easy to see where to join to at the end of the round.

Chain 2. Then the next 2 stitches are worked as back posts around the next 2 Round 10 stitches.

The red needle is between the 2 stitches needing a back post stitch.

Now, work a front post stitch around the one that gathered the 5 Round 9 stitches.

And 2 more back post stitches around the Round 10 stitches.

The red needle is between the 2 stitches needing a back post stitch.

Chain 2 and we're back to a front post stitch around the cluster.

> **THIS WAY**
>
> There should be a 2-chain space either side of the 5 post stitches between the clusters.

The needles are in the 2-chain spaces

R12

R13

Easy! Work a small stitch in every stitch and 2 in each 2-chain space.

R13

Reef Ripples Help

R14

Nothing hard here, You are alternating between working 7 tall stitches and single small stitches. Remember to chain 2 between the sets of stitches.

> **THIS WAY**
>
> Your small stitches should always fall in the stitch above the cluster and the 7 large stitches should be above the popcorns. There should be 10 fans of large stitches.

The red needle is in the stitch in a cluster and the silver needle is in the stitch in the popcorn.

R14

R15

There's an easy start with a small stitch in same stitch as slip stitch. Then you will be working 2 half stitches (encasing the 2-chain space) into the first two of four skipped stitches of Round 13.

> **THIS WAY**
>
> Make sure you encase the 2-chain space as you work your 2 half stitches where the needles are. Insert your hook as the needles are placed.

Now remember the first round of Coastal Sunrise where we worked a stitch, then worked 2 stitches around it? You do that in each of the next 7 stitches.

Next, work another 2 half stitches encasing the 2-chain space but this time into the last two of the four skipped stitches of Round 13.

Work a single small stitch into the next stitch. It may be a little obscured by your last stitch.

Again, encase the chain into the first two of four skipped stitches before working a back post stitch around the next 7 stitches.

Encase the 2-chain space with half stitches in the next 2 Round 13 stitches before you start again.

> **THIS WAY**
>
> At the end of the round, you will have 5 sets of 7 back post stitches and 5 sets of 7 2 stitches around one stitch.
>
> There should be 5 stitches between the shells.

R15

R16

Nothing too hard in this round. Like the previous round, you alternate between what you do for each shell.

After your first small stitch in the same stitch as your slip stitch was made, you crochet the next 2 stitches together.

Then, you work a small stitch into the back loop only of the 21 shell stitches.

In the dip, crochet the next 2 stitches together, work a stitch in the next stitch and crochet the next 2 stitches together.

There should be 3 stitches between the shells.

R16

Now work 2 stitches in each of the next 7 stitches.

R17

Once you make your first stitch, skip the next stitch and work a small stitch in the back loop only of the next 21 stitches again.

Work a single small stitch in the stitch in the dip between shells.

For the second shell, skip the first and last stitch and work a regular back post stitch around the 14 stitches between.

The stitches you skip are the 2-together stitches of Round 16.

Skip the stitches the silver needles are in

There should be 1 stitch between the shells.

R17

R18

The stitches either side of the stitch in the dip are skipped. The first and last stitches of each shell are skipped.

The first shell, you again work small stitches into the back loop only but this time just of 19 stitches. The second shell, you work a regular stitch into 12 stitches.

There is again 1 stitch in the dip between shells.

R18

R19

We are going to start to make our shape into a circle in this round, so there are a lot of different stitches used.

At the start, after chaining 4, the types of stitches worked into the back loops only of the first shell vary. The smallest stitches will be along the middle 5 stitches.

The stitch in the dip this time is a large stitch.

The second shell has a back post regular stitch worked around all 12 stitches.

R19

R20

And here we are at the last round of the Reef Ripples section of The Cove. All stitches are half stitches.

The chain 2 starting chain is the first stitch, then you work a half stitch in the back loop only of the first 9 stitches of the first shell. The middle stitch has 2 half stitches worked into it.

The next 9 have a half stitch worked into the back loop only. Then, it's 1 stitch in the middle one between the shells.

The next 12 stitches all have half stitches worked into them. There are 2 in each of the first three, 1 in each of the middle six stitches and 2 in each of the last three stitches.

Instead of joining with a slip stitch, this round ends with an invisible join so we get an unbroken line of "v"s.

To make an invisible join, cut the yarn after making your last half stitch. Pull it up through the top of the last stitch and thread it onto a yarn needle. Insert the needle under the top of the first real half stitch (the one after the chain 2 starting chain).

Then insert the needle into the top of the last stitch, the same place the tail is emerging from, also going through the loop under the "v".

Pull gently on the tail until the loop is the same size as the other stitches.

R20

Reef Ripples Help

Seashells

Round by round help

 Seashells video

 Seashells mirrored video

It's time to forage the shoreline for shells.

R21

As the yarn was cut at the end of Reef Ripples, you need to attach it at the start of this round. The best way to do that is with a standing stitch. Attach the yarn to your hook with a slip knot and make the stitch as you usually would. The only difference is you need to hold onto the loop on your hook or you will lose your yarn over.

 **Try this!**

You can use a standing stitch for any stitch. Be it small or large or part of a cluster of some description. A great trick if you are changing colours a lot.

Where you join and work all stitches of Round 21 may be new to you. Instead of working into the top of the stitches, you poke your hook into the loop behind the "v" of the stitch – or "lbv" as I call it. It is also known as the third loop.

Seashells Help

Once you have joined your yarn by working a regular stitch, work a stitch in the loop behind v of every stitch, all the way around. One regular stitch in every loop behind v.

The first stitches of the side are 2 large stitches in the next stitch and 3 large stitches in the next st.

R21

R22

This is the round we go from a rounded shape to one with four sides and corners.

> **THIS WAY**
>
> From now on, all stitch counts will describe one side and corner.

The corners of Round 22 are made with large stitches, so you begin with chain 4 as the starting chain or a false stitch, followed by a large stitch in the same stitch you joined into with a slip stitch at the end of Round 21.

Then, you skip 3 stitches. The silver needle on the left shows where to work the next side stitch.

> **THIS WAY**
>
> For a seamless look, corners with more than one stitch in them will begin with half of the stitches needed and the other half of the corner stitches will be made at the end of the round.

The side repeat between the tall stitches begins (and ends) with 2 small stitches. Easy. Now, remember the first Round and Round 15 where we worked 2 stitches around a stitch just made? Well, in this round we are doing the same thing but with 3 stitches worked around the one just made.

Then you skip 1 stitch and work a small stitch in the next. Do that 12 times in total along the side. You only skip a stitch between the 3 around 1 and the small stitch. You go straight from small stitch to regular stitch.

At the end of the side, you need to work 1 more small stitch before skipping 3 and working your large stitches.

The corner shape overall is all large stitches. 3, 2, 3, 2, 3 as shown in this picture. The silver needles show the 2-stitch sets.

After you have completed all of your corners and sides, you need to finish off the corner you started at the beginning of the round by working a large stitch in the same stitch as your first stitches.

Try this!

If you are not sure where to work into the same stitch or space as your first stitches, look where the first stitch you made after the starting chain or false stitch is worked. That's the spot!

R22

Seashells Help

R23

All of the corner stitches are used more than once. The middle corner stitch is used three times, while the stitches either side of it are used twice.

Again, we begin with chain 4 or a false stitch, then you work a front post tall stitch around the chain 4 starting chain (or false stitch) of Round 22.

The next 6 stitches are all used twice. Work a large stitch in the next stitch, then work a front post around the same stitch.

The first side stitch is a back post around the first base stitch of the sideways shells – the one the three stitches were worked around.

Then it's a simple matter of chaining 2 and moving across to the next base stitch. The 4 stitches you are skipping are the 3 around the base stitch and the small stitch.

 **THIS WAY**

There are no 2-chain spaces before the first and after the last back post stitch.

When you get to the large corner stitches, again you will be using each stitch twice, but in a different order. You work a front post tall stitch first, then a tall stitch in that same stitch.

Seashells Help

If you find it tricky to see where to work into the same stitch, pull your front post stitch down to expose the top of the stitch.

The middle corner stitch is used three times. Around, in and around again.

The very last stitch of the round is a front post tall stitch around the same stitch the first front post stitch was worked around.

R23

R24

The corners are simple enough with a small stitch in the first 9 stitches, then crochet 2 stitches together, skip the 2 last tall stitches and the first back post stitch before you start the side.

The side stitches are worked into Rounds 22 and 23. The first stitch of the side is worked into the loop behind v of a Round 22 stitch. The stitch you want is the first of the 3 worked around a stitch. The loop behind v should be sitting right up the top, ready for you.

The side is easy from here. Work 2 regular stitches into the 2-chain space of Round 23 then back to the loop behind v of the Round 22 stitch. You skip the back post stitch between the 2-chain spaces.

The side finishes with a stitch in the loop behind v of the last Round 22 shell. Then you skip the back post stitch and the first 2 tall corner stitches and crochet the next 2 stitches together.

R24

R25

Again, the corners are nothing challenging. The sides are where the interesting bits are.

> **THIS WAY**
>
> The last and first back loop only corner stitches should fall in the 2-together stitch.

Now the side. You begin by crocheting 4 stitches together, then you make double crossed stitches. These crosses are made by skipping 1 stitch, working 2 stitches in the next stitch, then working 2 stitches in the stitch you skipped.

The red needle is where to work the first 2 stitches and the silver needle shows where the second 2 stitches go.

> **THIS WAY**
>
> Be careful reading your stitches as it can be easy to not skip a stitch. You should have 13 double cross stitches along each side.

At the end of the side, you crochet 4 stitches together.

The corners are all 3 stitches in the corner stitch of Round 24.

R25

Seashells Help

R26

A nice quick round for you. Corners are easy. Once you get to the side, instead of working into stitches, you work a small stitch between all the double crosses and chain 2 between those small stitches.

There is no chain 2 between the first and last between double cross stitches.

The corners are a small stitch, chain 2 and a small stitch in the middle corner stitch.

Try this!

Some rounds end with the instruction to join with a stitch other than a slip stitch. Most often in this pattern it is a single crochet. This single crochet join means your yarn is in the very point of a corner – the exact right spot to begin the next round. Treat the joining stitch the same as a chain space. When you are instructed to work a stitch over the joining stitch, put your hook in the corner space so you encase the joining stitch, just like you would a chain space.

It can help to pop a scrap of yarn in the gap before you join. This scrap of yarn shows you where to work a stitch over the joining stitch and also the last stitch of the round.

Seashells Help

R26

R27

Now it's time to create some shells along the sides. Around the corner stitches, you chain 1 and skip 1, working a small stitch in the next st.

The beginning and end of the sides have 2 small stitches next to each other.

Along the side, after the second small stitch in a stitch (red needle), you will only be using the 2-chain spaces. In the first one, you work 5 regular stitches and the next, a single small stitch.

You should end with 5 stitches in the last 2-chain space.

Seashells Help

The corners for this round are 1 small stitch in the 2-chain corner space.

R28

OK! Here we go with some fun!

Around the corner shapes, you will be working puff stitches into the 1-chain spaces and a regular stitch into the stitches. The corner is 1 stitch in the corner stitch.

Along the sides, you will be doing the same thing when you get to the shells for the next few rounds.

The first shell has a small stitch worked into the loop behind v of the first 3 stitches. You skip 1 stitch at the start and end of the side.

R28

Seashells Help

Moving along the side, work 5 regular stitches into the small stitch between the shells, then a small stitch in the loop behind v of the middle stitch of the next shell.

R28

R29

Around the corner shapes, you will be using the puff stitches twice. First you work a stitch in it (the hole on the right - left for left handers) and then a front post stitch around it. Previously when we have done this, on the other side of the corner shape, the order of front post and stitch in has been reversed. Not this time! All puff stitches are used the same way – a stitch in, then a stitch around.

Along the side, after skipping 1 stitch and working a small stitch in the next 2 stitches, the sides are the same with the treatment of the shells. 3 stitches in the loop behind v of the first shell, 5 regular stitches in the dip between shells and a stitch in the loop behind v of the middle shell stitch. And you finish with a small stitch in the loop behind v of the last 3 stitches of the last shell.

The corners this time are again a small stitch, chain 2 and another small stitch in the corner stitch.

Seashells Help

R29

R30

There is nothing new in this round. You have done everything before. It's just the numbers that are different.

The corners are 1 stitch in the 2-chain corner space.

R30

Seashells Help

R31

Small stitches in the back loop only around the corner shapes and then the same as the last 2 rounds along the sides with less shells.

The corners are small stitch, chain 2 and a small stitch in the corner stitch.

R31

R32

The stitches around the corner shapes are like what you did in Round 25 with the double cross shapes. This time, the crosses are made with 2 stitches in total.

Skip 1 stitch, work a stitch in the next stitch (red needle), then work a stitch in the skipped stitch (silver needle)

There is nothing new along the sides. You can do it. The thing to note is when it's time to work your first cross stitch, you skip 2 stitches.

R33

This is the last of the shells along the side rounds. You have done all the stitches and techniques before. A nice quick round.

R32

R33

Seashells Help

R34

This is the round where the shape becomes more square. After the initial stitches in the back loop only around the corner shapes, the side stitches are worked into stitches. There are different sized stitches to fill in the shape.

> **THIS WAY**
>
> Make sure your slip stitches are not tight. This will help work into them in the next round.

The middle side stitches are slip stitches into the loop behind v of the last shell.

R34

R35

The last round of the Seashells section. And it's an easy one. The corners are 2 stitches, chain 2 and 2 more stitches worked into the 2-chain corner space.

R35

Seashells Help

Wickerwork
Round by round help

 Wickerwork video

 Wickerwork mirrored video

Time to relax. Imagine yourself with a lovely cool drink, relaxing in a gorgeous wickerwork peacock chair.

R36

We kick things off with a small stitch round where all the stitches along the sides are worked into the back loops only. The corners are the usual 1 stitch, chain 2, 1 stitch.

R36

R37

Before you get too comfortable, let's get the next couple of rounds of interesting things done before you kick back and flow.

The start and corners are easy. After you skip the first stitch, the sides instruction may make you worry. It's ok. You can do it.

The side stitches are 4 stitches crocheted together. The interesting part is you work 2 legs into one stitch, skip the next stitch and work the last 2 legs in the next stitch.

Begin 2 stitches where the red needle is, skipping the stitch where the silver needle is.

Then skip 1 stitch and begin 2 stitches in the next stitch before finishing off your together stitch.

R38

Nothing too hard here – all small stitches with some spike stitches along the sides.

The spike stitches are worked into the Round 36 stitch you skipped in the middle of the 4-together stitches in Round 37.

R37

R38

Wickerwork Help

R39

A regular stitch round! The first stitch of each side is skipped, otherwise, it's just a regular stitch in every stitch.

Skip the stitch with the silver needle

The corners are 3 stitches in the 2-chain corner spaces.

R39

R40

Relax. A small stitch round.

R40

R41

The sides have 4 stitches crocheted together, as well as small stitches and chains. The together stitches are regular ones this time. Start a stitch in 4 stitches before crocheting them together.

The corners are a little different as they are a single stitch in the 2-chain corner space.

R41

The corners have 5 stiches in the 1 corner stitch.

R42

The sides are where the action is. The small stitches have 4 regular stitches worked into them. Each of the together stitches has a small stitch worked into it.

R42

R43

The last interesting round before you can relax and take it easy for a while.

Between chains along the side, you will be working front post and back post stitches alternately around Round 41 stitches.

The first front post stitch is around the 4-together stitch.

The first back post stitch is worked around the Round 41 stitch with 4 stitches in it from Round 42.

You ignore all Round 42 stitches until the end of the side where you work a small stitch in each of the last 2 stitches.

The red needle indicates the middle corner stitch where the Round 43 corner is worked.

R43

R44

Relax time. This round is all small stitches in all stitches and 2 in each 2-chain space along the side.

R44

R45

A regular stitch round, with the first side stitch skipped and 3-stitch corners. Nothing new.

R45

R46

Small stitch round. Easy!

R46

R47

The same as Round 45. You've got this.

R47

R48

A little bit interesting, but not hard.

Along the side, you will alternate between working a front post stitch around the next stitch and a stitch in the next stitch. The corners are 3 stitches.

R49, 50 and 51

These rounds are the same as Round 48. Along the sides, you will always be working a stitch in stitch first, then a front post stitch. The front posts are always around a stitch in a stitch and the stitch in next stitch are always in front post stitches.

R48

 THIS WAY

There will always be 5 stitches around the corners between the front post stitches.

R49

Note: R50 and R51 are not shown.

R52

A small stitch round.

R52

R53

A regular stitch round with 3-stitch corners.

R53

R54

One more small stitch round to finish the Wickerwork section off.

R54

Cabana Days
Round by round help

 Cabana Days video

 Cabana Days mirrored video

After a long stroll, it's nice to laze about the pool with a good book or cocktail.

R55

We'll start off easy with V stitches along the sides made of 1 stitch, chain 1 and another stitch in the same stitch. Even the corners are V stitches worked into the 2-chain corner spaces.

R55

Cabana Days Help

R56

The corners are 3 stitches in the 1-chain corner space with a front post stitch worked around the corner stitches either side.

The side V stitches are used to crochet 2 stitches together – you ignore the 1-chain space in the middle of the V stitch. The together stitches are worked as front post stitches.

Begin a front post stitch around each of the stitches before finishing the stitch.

R56

R57

For a few rounds, we'll be doing more things either side of the corners to create some cool shapes.

After starting and your first 2 front post stitches, we begin the side repeat. There are 3 stitches in the repeat.

After you work a small stitch in the 1-chain space, work a tall stitch behind the work into a stitch of Round 54 – the one skipped in the V stitch round. Every one of the skipped Round 54 stitches is used.

Fold work down to work a tall stitch behind.

Then work a front post small stitch around the together stitch.

Cabana Days Help

The end of the side finishes with a tall stitch behind in the last skipped stitch of Round 54.

> **THIS WAY**
>
> Don't worry about the big loopy tops of the tall stitches. They won't be visible after the next round.

R57

R58

All small stiches in this round and a lot of them are 2-together stitches.

There are 3 stitches in the side repeat – 2-together, skip 1, 2-together, stitch in next. So you are skipping every second front post stitch and working a stitch into the alternate front posts.

The red needle is in the skipped front post stitch and the silver one is in the front post stitch with a stitch worked into it.

R58

R59

For the next few rounds, all the interesting action will be around the corners. The sides are easy.

> **THIS WAY**
>
> Before you begin, take a moment to identify the first and last front post stitches of each side of Round 57. Pop a stitch marker around them to make them stand out.

The next part feels like you are working forwards then back.

After your first stitch over the joining stitch, you work a front post stitch around the first front post stitch of Round 57 to the left (right for left handers). Then, you work a regular stitch in the second stitch of Round 58, behind the front post you just made.

The red needle is where you work the next front post stitch. The silver is where you work the next regular stitch into the next Round 58 stitch. No stitches are skipped this time.

Now it's time for the sides – easy! A half stitch in the next 103 stitches. You should have 2 unworked stitches of Round 58 left at this point.

You are working forwards and backwards again.

The red needle shows where to work your regular stitch and the silver needle, where to work the first front post stitch.

Repeat with the next stitch of Round 58 and a front post around the last front post of Round 57.

Cabana Days Help

The corners of this round are a small stitch in the 2-chain corner space.

R59

R60

The corner stitch of Round 60 is not worked into the corner stitch of Round 59. We ignore that corner stitch completely.

The corner stitch is a front post stitch around the 2 front post stitches either side of that corner stitch. Here is where to work the first one.

Now, work 2 stitches into the next stitch. The next unworked stitch will be a front post stitch and we will use it three times.

First work a front post stitch around it, then work 2 stitches into it.

You may need to fold the front post stitch down to see where to work the 2 stitches.

The last stitch before you begin the half stiches along the side should be worked into the last regular stitch before the half stitches of Round 59.

The side stitches are again 103 half stiches worked into the loop behind v of the half stitches.

After your 103 half stitches, the next stitch should be a regular stitch. Work a regular stitch into it.

The next stitch will be a front post stitch. First, work 2 stitches into it, then 1 around it.

Now work 2 regular stitches in the next stitch. Then it's time for the front post corner stitch around the 2 front post stitches either side of the corner stitch we are ignoring.

R60

R61

This is the last round where the sides are the same 103 half stiches in the loop behind v.

At the start, you will use the same stitch as slip stitch (the front post corner stitch) twice. First, work the starting chain or a false stitch, then a front post stitch around the front post corner stitch.

Now, work a regular stitch in the next 4 stitches. The next stitch is a front post stitch around the front post below, a little to the right (left for left handers). It is the stitch with the third of the 4 regular stitches in it.

The last 2 stitches before the half stiches have a regular stitch worked into them.

Those 103 side stitches have a half stitch worked into the loop behind v again for the last time.

Next work a regular stitch into the next 2 regular stitches. Now work a front post stitch around the front post stitch a little to the left (right for left handers).

Work a stitch in each of the next 4 stitches before the corner. You may need to fold the front post stitch down to expose where to work the first 2 of these 4 stitches.

In the corner, we use the front post corner stitch of Round 60 three times. Around, in and around again.

The very last stitch of the round is a front post stitch around the same stitch a front post was worked around at the beginning.

R61

R62

Time to start a new thing along the sides! The front post stitches of Round 61 will be used twice.

At the start of the round, the first front post stitch has a stitch worked into it then around it.

After a stitch in the next 4, you use the next stitch twice, once in and then around.

The last 2 regular stitches are crocheted together.

Along the side, work a stitch in the loop behind v of the next 3 stitches, chain 1, skip 1 stitch. Repeat that all along the side. The last 3 half stiches should have a stitch worked into the loop behind v.

Next, you crochet the next 2 stitches together, before using the front post stitch twice. This time by working a stitch around it first then 1 in the same stitch.

After a stitch is worked in the next 4 stitches, treat the next front post stitch the same way – a stitch around it then in it.

The corners are 3 stitches in the corner stitch.

R62

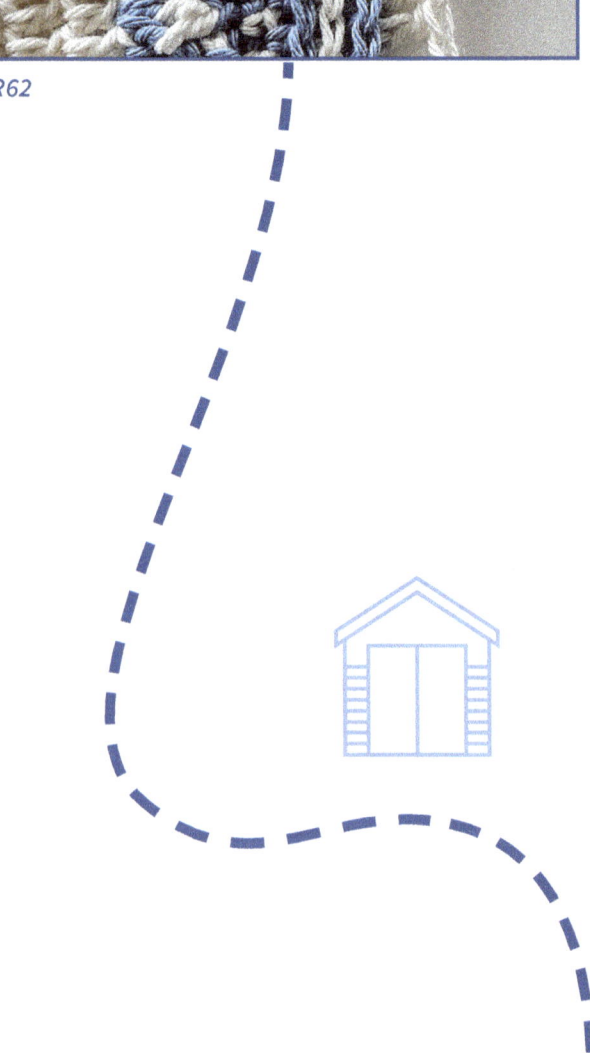

R63

Now we move from interesting corners to interesting sides. After starting with a small stitch in the same stitch as the slip stitch, and 1 in the next 2 stitches, there is a front post stitch, 5 back post stitches and another front post stitch.

> **THIS WAY**
>
> The 5 back post stitches should fall between front post stitches at the start and end of each side.

The 2-together stitch of Round 62 is skipped and the first of 3 stitches worked into the loop behind v has a small stitch worked into it. Then the middle of the 3 stitches has a front post stitch worked around it.

The last set of 3 stitches has a small stitch worked into the last stitch after the front post stitch.

The silver needle shows where to work the front post stitch before the 5 back post stitches.

From here, along the side, each 1-chain space has 5 regular stitches worked into it. The middle stitch of the 3 worked into the loop behind v has a front post small stitch worked around it.

R63

Cabana Days Help

R64

After the small stitch in the same stitch as the slip stitch, work a small stitch in the next 10 stitches. The red needle is in the first and the silver in the last of the 10 stitches.

Now you will begin working between Rounds 63 and 61. The front post stitches of Round 63 will all have a front post stitch worked around them.

Between working those front posts, work 3 tall stitches into the loop behind v of the stitches you skipped of Round 61. They were skipped in Round 62. Before you begin, identify the stitch you need the loop behind v of.

It may help to fold the work towards you to work the 3 tall stitches in that loop behind v.

R64

R65

As you need to end this round with an invisible join, if you have been working false stitch, don't do that this time. Work chain 3.

After the regular stitches in 4 stitches, you will be dipping down to the 5 Round 63 back post stitches to work a back post around them.

The next 2 stitches are small ones where the needles are in this photo:

Now, we begin the side repeat.

The front post stitches have a slip stitch worked into them.

THIS WAY

> The slip stitches along the side are included in the stitch count.

You can do the bits between the slip stitches – 2 half stitches in the first and last of the three and 3 half stitches in the middle stitch.

After your last slip stitch, work a small stitch in the next 2 stitches.

Then, work your 5 back post stitches around the back post stitches of Round 63.

At the end of the round, just like in Round 20, end with an invisible join.

R65

R66

To begin, attach your yarn by working a standing back post stitch around the middle stitch of any corner.

Along the side, you will be alternating what you do with each of the fans. The first fan has a small stitch worked in the loop behind v of the 7 fan stitches.

For the next fan, you work back post stitches around the 3 Round 64 tall stitches and skip the half stitches and slip stitches.

The red needle is pointing to the 3 tall stitches to work a back post stitch around. The silver needle is in the first stitch of 9 to skip before going back to a small stitch in the loop behind v of 7 stitches.

R66

R67

R67

There is only one interesting part of this round. When you work your 6 tall stitches together stitch, you work 2 legs in 3 stitches instead of 1 leg in 6 stitches.

These clusters are always worked into the 3 back post stitches of Round 66.

R68

A nice easy round of mostly small stitches. You will skip the 1-chain spaces either side of the clusters and work a front post stitch around the clusters.

R68

Cabana Days Help

R69

You don't need me for this one. A small stitch round.

R69

R70

The interesting parts happen around the corners.

Begin with chain 4 then, work a 4-tall stitch together stitch, with the first 2 legs over the joining stitch and the next 2 in the first 2 stitches.

> **THIS WAY** ▶
>
> If you are using false stitches, you can begin a tall false stitch and make a full 5-stitch cluster at the beginning.

Cabana Days Help

At the end of the side, you will work a 5-tall stitch together stitch over the last 2 stitches and the 2-chain corner space. 1 leg in each of the last 2 stitches and 3 legs in the 2-chain corner space.

R71

At the start, after working your starting chain or false stitch, work 3 tall stitches over the joining stitch.

At the end of this round, you will join with a stitch, not a small stitch this time, but a regular stitch (treble UK, double US).

The clusters are skipped, as is the first stitch of the side.

R70

R71

Cabana Days Help

R72

The tall stitches around the corner are all used twice. At the start of the side, you work a small stitch in the stitch and then a front post small stitch around the same stitch.

Over the next 4 stitches (worked in the 4-chain space of Round 71), you crochet 2-together, twice.

This is the second lot of 2 stitches to crochet together.

Now we come to the side. Every stitch along the side is used. First, work a small stitch in the next stitch, chain 2 and then crochet the next 2 stitches together, using the back loops only.

Chain 2 and work a small stitch in the next stitch. When you get to the four stitches worked into the 4-chain space, crochet 2-together again twice.

The tall stitches are all used twice. This time by working a front post small stitch first, followed by a small stitch in the same stitch. You may need to pull the front post stitch down to expose the top of the stitch to work into.

R72

R73

Are you ready for a ruffly round? The path will be smoother the next round I promise.

There's nothing hard, just a lot of stitches along the sides.

The 2-together stitches have a small stitch worked into them. There is no chain before the first one of these stitches.

Then, chain 2 and work 5 regular stitches into the small stitch between the 2-together stitches.

There is a 2-chain space between each small stitch and set of 5 regular stitches in one.

After chaining 2 and working a small stitch in the next st, go straight to working 5 tall stitches into the small stitch.

There is no chain 2 either side of the 5 tall stitches.

There is no chain 2 before you start the 11 regular stitches before the corner.

R73

Cabana Days Help

R74

Time to smooth the path, turning some of those sets of 5 stitches into popcorns.

The sides begin with a variety of front post stitches. It will be clear if you are on track.

Once you get to the side, what you do with each set of 5 stitches will alternate. The small stitches will always have a small stitch worked into them.

The first set of 5 regular stitches, you gather together by working 1 small stitch in the two 2-chain spaces either side of the 5 stitches. Insert your hook as the red needle shows.

After working that gathering stitch, work a small stitch in the next stitch, and then a front post stitch around the 5 tall stitches.

R74

R75

This is a long stretch of path. It's not rough, but will take some time.

Mostly, it is a stitch in every stitch. Until you get to those 5 front post stitches. Each of those needs a picot in them.

 **Try This!**

Traditionally, a picot is made of a small stitch, some chains and then a slip stitch into the small stitch or first chain. It can be really fiddly and annoying to do. Instead, I work a small stitch into the small stitch. Much easier, and they sit better too!

Work a small stitch into the small stitch made at the start of the picot.

The side is a repeat of 5 picots then a small stitch in the next 3 stitches. The middle of the 3 small stitches should fall above the gathering popcorn stitch.

R75

R76

More fun! The sides are the interesting parts.

Remember the 3 small stitches over the popcorns? Well, you will crochet those 3 together.

Next, identify the 5 stitches of Round 73 behind all those picots. They are the ones you worked a front post stitch around. You will need to fold the picot part down.

Each of those 5 stitches has a stitch worked into it. You won't really see them from the front.

The corners of this round are a single small stitch in the 2-chain corner space.

R76

R77

Almost there! This is the last round with an interesting bit for Cabana Days.

You will be fine until you come to the back post stitch around the "next stitch and the picot of Round 75 at the same time".

First, identify the next stitch and the middle of the 5 picots.

Now, insert your hook from the back up through both layers.

And down the other side to work your back post stitch. This anchors the frilly picot part to the base.

Here's what it looks like with front posts either side of it, with the picots folded down and then as it sits.

Again the corner is a single small stitch in the corner stitch of Round 76.

R77

R78

And sweet relief. The end is in sight. A variety of stitches, but just 1 in each stitch with nothing fancy happening.

R78

R79

The end of the Cabana Days path! A simple small stitch round.

How you end this round depends on where you want to go next.

If you're taking the short cut to Pebble Beach, end with chain 1 and join with a small stitch so you can continue on.

If the scenic route is calling you, end with chain 2 and a slip stitch.

R79

Pebble Beach
Round by round help

 Pebble Beach video

 Pebble Beach mirrored video

Whether you got here via the short cut or scenic route, the path from here is the same after the set-up.

If you took the **Short Cut**, follow the rounds labelled **SC**, if you took the **Scenic Route**, follow the rounds labelled **SR**.

> ▎THIS WAY ▶
>
> If you have been dreading Pebble Beach because you thought it was made of crochet bobbles, you can relax. Sure they look like bobbles, but they are not – and they are really easy to do!

R80 SR only

This is the set-up round for the Pebble Beach border. The last round of Cabana Days was a round of small stitches. So just for the Scenic Route, you need to do the same.

As you get to the joins of the small squares, work a stitch in each chain space and join.

R80 SR

Pebble Beach Help

R80 SC R81 SR

This is an easy one! It is a regular stitch round.

> **THIS WAY**
>
> If you have followed the short cut, skip the first stitch of each side so you have an odd number of stitches along each side.

R80 SC/R81 SR

R81 SC R82 SR

Nice and easy! Small stitches, 2-chain spaces and skipping 1 stitch as you work along the side.

R81 SC/R82 SR

R82 SC R83 SR

We begin to make the bobble-like stitches in this round. They won't look like bobbles until you do the next round.

At the start and end of the sides, there is a together stitch worked over the 2-chain space and a stitch.

After working the corner stitches, the first crochet 3-together stitch is made with 1 leg in the next stitch and 2 legs in the 2-chain space.

Along the side, skip all the small stiches and work a 3-stitch cluster in each of the 2-chain spaces and chain 2 between them.

At the end of the side, work another 3-together stitch, with the first 2 legs in the last 2-chain space of the side and 1 leg in the last stitch.

There is no chain space before the first or after the last 3-together stitch, so the corners look like 5 stitches – 3 in the 2-chain corner space and a stitch either side.

R82 SC/R83 SR

R83 SC R84 SR

Now the magic happens! The bobble-like shapes are formed by working a spike stitch between the clusters and a front post stitch around the clusters.

The spike stitches are worked into the skipped stitch of Rounds 81-82 (skipped in Rounds 82-83). Every skipped stitch has a spike stitch worked into it.

Poke your hook just like how the red needle is inserted. You will be encasing the 2-chain space as you work the spike stitch.

> **THIS WAY**
>
> Usually when I give tips on making spike stitches, I recommend lifting up a long loop. In this case, the shorter your spike stitch, the poppier your faux bobble will be.

Then, work a front post stitch around the 3-together stitch.

Pebble Beach Help

R83 SC/R84 SR

84 SC 85 SR

Now it's time to start the next round of pebbles. It is almost the same as the last round. This time, there will be 9 stitches around the corner – 3 in the 2-chain corner space and 3 each side of it.

The 3-stitch clusters will always be made in the spike stitches and you will always skip the front post stitches along the side.

84 SC/85 SR

R85 SC R86 SR

You have done all this before. The difference is more stitches around the corners.

One thing to look out for is not to skip the first stitch after the last front post stitch on the side.

Repeat the last 2 rounds once more. Or more times if you have extra yarn and want to make the border wider.

They are not pictured.

R85 SC/R86 SR

R88 SC R89 SR

An easy small stitch round and you are all done!

R88 SC/R89 SR

Pebble Beach Help

Small Patterns
Round by round help

If you've already made The Cove up to the end of Cabana Days, you will likely not need this help section. These smaller patterns were designed using features of the main Cove blanket. Rather than repeat help already given, I mention the relevant rounds in the following help so you can refer to them if you do need a spot of direction.

Sunset Shells

The first 6 rounds are the same as Coastal Sunrise. The help for these rounds is on page 60.

 Sunset Shells video

 Sunset Shells mirrored video

R7

A squaring off round, different stitches, but an easy round of a stitch in each stitch. The corners are 3 tall stitches.

R7

132   Small Patterns Help

R8

Super easy! A small stitch round.

R8

R9

The only thing to watch out for here is to skip 2 at the end of the side instead of skipping 3 as you do along the side.

R9

Small Patterns Help

R10

Ok now the fun begins! This is basically the same as Round 27 of the Seashells section, with less shells along the side. The help for Round 27 is on page 86.

The first stitch of the side is worked into the loop behind v of the first stitch of the first side shell.

R10

R11

Along the sides, this round is the same as Round 28 of the Seashells section. The help for Round 28 is on page 87.

The corners though are shells of 5 stitches in the 2-chain corner spaces. There is also a regular stitch in a stitch either side of the corner, making it look like there are 7 stitches around the corner.

R11

R12

Again, this is much the same as Round 29 of the Seashells section. The help for Round 29 is on page 88.

R12

R13

Another round similar to the last one. You can do it!

R13

R14

And we finish off with a small stitch round, with the side stitches worked into the back loop only. Easy!

R14

Ripples

While the stitches and techniques used in the Ripples pattern are relatively easy, you will need to pay attention to make sure you are working the right technique in the right spot.

 Ripples video

 Ripples mirrored video

R1

Such an easy start. A round of 16 stitches.

> **THIS WAY**
>
> It really will pay to check your stitch count when working this pattern or your ripples may turn into a whirlpool.

R1

R2

There are six stitches between the * and ** asterisks. The middle 2 are worked into the back loop only, while the 2 stitches either side are worked into the stitches.

> **THIS WAY**
>
> Even though we are working in the round, the instructions are similar to if you were making a square. The stitch/es after the ** are kind of like corners in a square.

R2

R3

The "side" stitches are either worked as back posts or into the back loop only. The back post stitches are worked around the 2 stitches in 1 stitch. The stitches to be worked into the back loop only are worked into the stitches that were worked into the back loop themselves.

The "corner" stitches are worked into stitches as normal.

At the end of the round, work another stitch into the same stitch as the first stitch.

R3

R4

The "side" stitches are either worked into stitches as normal, or into the back loop only. Back loops of the ones in back loops.

The difference is there are 2 worked in one stitch then 1 in the next.

The "corner" stitches are 2 stitches in each stitch.

Here is one repeat completed.

R4

R5

Much the same as Round 3, but with more stitches along the "side".

The "corners" are a stitch in each stitch.

R5

R6

This round will feel different, but the same thing is happening. You will be working stitches into the back loops only of the stiches worked into back loops again. The rest of the stitches are simply a stitch in every stitch.

2 stitches in the back loop only where the silver needles are and 1 in the back loop only where the red needle is.

R6

R7

You know what you're doing by now. We are back to back posts and back loop only stitches around the "sides" and stitches in stitches in the "corners".

R7

R8

Now, it's time to square off our circle. Hooray. Real corners and sides from here on in.

It's a regular squaring off round with different sized stitches. The difference is some are worked into the back loop only. You guessed it – into the back loops only of the stitches worked into the back loops only.

The corners are a little different as well. Instead of all 4 corner stitches being worked into the one stitch, 2 are worked into 2 stitches with a chain space between them.

R8

R9

Back posts and back loops only again along the side. Nothing hard.

R9

R10

Most stitches are in the next stitch, except the ones in the back loop only in the middle of the side.

R10

R11

A small stitch round, worked into the back loop only along the sides.

R11

Fans

The fan-like parts of this pattern are the same as the early parts of the Wickerwork section.

R1

Clusters, chains and regular stitches make up Round 1.

R1

Small Patterns Help

R2

A small stitch round, with front posts worked around the 4-together stitches and 2 in each 2-chain space.

R2

R3

A quick square off round.

R3

R4

So easy – a small stitch round.

R4

R5

Now the fun begins! Set up for the fan-like section. Every stitch along the sides is used.

R5

R6

Nothing hard here. When you get to the 4-together stitches, this is where you work the stitch into it.

The 4 stitches in one are worked into the small stitch in the middle of the side.

R6

R7

This round gives the fans their slightly puffy look by working front and back post stitches.

The first front post stitch is worked around the 4-together stitch of Round 5.

After chaining 1, the back post stitch is worked around the Round 5 stitch that has 4 stitches in it.

Then, you chain 1 and work another front post stitch around the next 4-together stitch of Round 5.

R7

R8

A nice easy one for you.

R8

R9

This round is much the same as Round 5 but with 5-together stitches. The thing to note is the chain spaces at the start and end of the sides are made of 2 chains. The chain spaces between the 5-together stitches are 3-chain spaces.

R9

R10

And this round is just like Round 6, with more fans and 5 stitches between the 5-together stitches of Round 9.

R10

Small Patterns Help

R11

The same technique of a front post around the 5-together stitch and a back post around the stitch with 5 stitches in it as you did in Round 7.

R11

R12

Just regular stitches in this round. Note there are 2 stitches worked into the back and front post stitches.

R12

R13

A small stitch round with all the sides stitches worked into the back loop only.

R13

R14

Exactly the same as Round 13, except for the end with chain 2 and a slip stitch join.

R14

Wicker

The easiest of the four small patterns. Rounds 7 to 12 are the same as the Rounds 48 to 54 of the Wickerwork section of the Cove. The help for those rounds is on page 100.

Wicker video
Wicker mirrored video

R1

The chain 1 at the start of Round 1 does not count in the stitch count. It is there to help make it easier to find the first small stitch to join into. Still, I recommend you place a stitch marker in the first small stitch as soon as you make it so there is no mistaking which is the first stitch to join into.

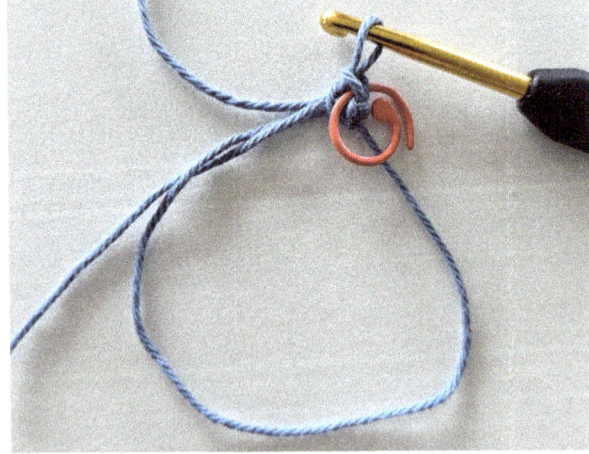

R1

R2

Just a regular stitch in 1 stitch and 2 in the next, all the way around.

R2

R3

A small stitch round, alternating between 2 stitches in a stitch, and 1 in the next 2 stitches.

R3

R4

A little square is the result of this round.

R4

R5

A small stitch round.

R5

R6

A regular stitch round, with 3 stitches in each 2-chain corner space.

R6

R7

Now the fun begins with the sides stitches alternating between a stitch in the next stitch and a front post stitch worked around the next stitch.

R7

R8

The same as Round 7, but with extra stitches along the side.

R8

R9

And the same again…

R9

R10

A small stitch round.

R10

R11

A tall stitch round.

R11

R12

Finish with a small stitch round.

R12

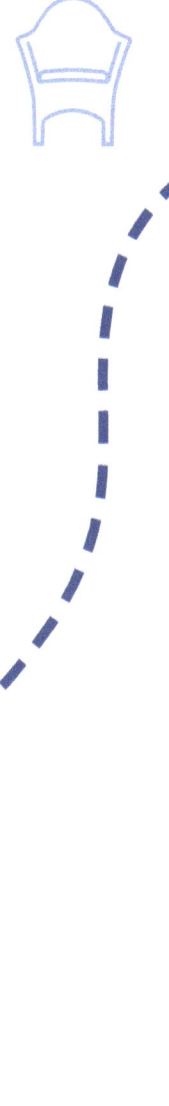

Small Patterns Help

Glossary

Abbreviations

cnr/s	corner/s	
R	round	
rep	repeat	
sp/s	space/s	
st/s	stitch/es	
stch	starting chain	Used in place of the first st in a round. Is included in st count.
stdg	standing	Attach yarn to your hook with a slip knot then work the st indicated as normal.
yo	yarn over	Wrap yarn over hook from back to front.

Stitches US

·	**ss**	slip stitch	Insert hook into st or sp indicated, yo and pull through st or sp and loop on hook.
o	**ch**	chain	yo, pull through loop on hook.
+	**sc**	single crochet	Insert hook into st or sp indicated, yo, pull loop to front, yo, pull through both loops on hook.
T	**hdc**	half double crochet	Wrap yarn around hook, insert hook into st or sp indicated, yo, pull loop to front (3 loops on hook), yo, pull through all 3 loops on hook.
✝	**dc**	double crochet	Wrap yarn around hook, insert hook into st or sp indicated, yo, pull loop to front (3 loops on hook), 2x [yo, pull through 2 loops on hook].
✝	**htr**	half triple crochet	Wrap yarn around hook twice, insert hook into st or sp indicated, yo, pull loop to front (4 loops on hook), yo, pull through 2 loops (3 loops on hook), yo, pull through all 3 loops on hook.
✝	**tr**	triple crochet	Wrap yarn around hook twice, insert hook into st or sp indicated, yo, pull loop to front (4 loops on hook), 3x [yo, pull through 2 loops].

Techniques

		at the same time	Shows where to place your hook when gathering sts from a previous round into one.
		behind	The bend in the post of the st shows it is worked behind previous round/s.
	blo	back loop only	Insert hook into the back loop only of the st indicated.
	bp	back post	Insert hook around the post of the st indicated from the back. Can be applied to any st.
	cl	cluster	Numerous sts worked together as one st in the st or sp indicated. Begin the type of st indicated as many times as instructed. Work each st of the cl up to before the last yo and pull through 2 loops on hook, then yo and pull though all loops on hook. Could be any number of any kind of st. e.g. 4trcl, 5dtrcl, 3htrcl and worked as fp or bp.
	fp	front post	Insert hook around the post of the st indicated from the front. Can be applied to any st.
		in front	The bend in the post of the st shows it is worked in front of previous round/s.
	inv join	invisible join	Cut yarn after completing last st of round. Pull tail up through the last st, thread tail onto needle, insert needle under "v" of first true st of the round and back through the centre of the last st, and through the lbv of the last st. Pull tight enough to form a "v" on top of the stch, weave end away.
	lbv	loop behind v	The third loop or back bump of a st on the back. It's located under the back loop of a st. Any st can be worked into lbv, including cl and tog sts.
	mc	magic circle	Method used to begin a square. Wrap yarn around a few fingers, forming a loop, insert your hook into the centre and pull the working yarn through, ch1 to secure. Work R1 sts into the ring, pull the tail to close the ring once all sts have been made and secure by weaving the end in well.
		picot	sc in next st, ch3, sc in sc just made.
	puff	puff stitch	3x [yo, insert hook into sp indicated, pull loop up] (7 loops on hook), yo, pull through all loops on hook.
	spike sc	spike single crochet	Insert hook into st or sp indicated, usually in a round more than 1 round prior to the current round, pull up a long loop level with the current round and work st as normal.
	tog	together	Numerous sts worked together as one st over a number of sts or sps as indicated. Work the specified number of sts up to before the last yo and pull through 2 loops on hook, then yo and pull though all loops on hook. "tog" will be followed by "over next # sts". It can be done with different numbers and types of sts. e.g. tr5tog over next 5 sts, dc2tog over next 2 sts. Can be worked as fp or bp.

Glossary

Helpful Links

Welcome to the download page, with some additional resources to complement your trip around The Cove.

To access the downloads, simply follow the provided links or scan the QR codes.

 Map

 Left-handed versions of the charts

 The Cove Taster Pattern

 The yarn needs for the four small squares

 Digital version of this book

Thank You

The Cove Crochet Blanket pattern, my 9th book, is a collective achievement, much like a crochet pattern with the threads of collaboration with many. Sure, I designed it, and I loved that part, but the making of that scribbled pattern into the lovely Cove you have to enjoy happened with the help of many fabulous folks.

Thank you, Michelle Lorimer. Your creative skills have given the book a look that perfectly complements The Cove pattern. Your design work has added so much depth to the experience of making The Cove.

As always, Amy Gunderson has created truly beautiful charts to accompany your trek around The Cove. They are works of art. Thank you, Amy.

To my technical editor and proofreader, SiewBee Pond, thank you once again for your keen eye and attention to detail which helped my words shine.

Thank you, Kelly Lonergan, for your expert chart tech editing and helping me with a real conundrum in the pattern writing process.

Thank you, Jo O'Keefe, for your stunning photography! You always know how to style my blankets so well. Thank you also to Jacinta for letting us take photos in your gorgeous house by the sea.

The fabulous blanket options for The Cove are only here because of some truly wonderful folks who devoted a lot of time to the making. Thank you, Kym Craswell, for making the baby blanket and Chris Wilkins for making the pink short cut blanket. A huge thank you to Kim Siebenhausen for choosing the colours and making the colourful scenic route blanket.

A special mention goes to the team of testers who tested the patterns and charts so well. Your assistance has been so helpful in making sure the pattern is easy to understand. Thank you, Anne, Bonita, Chantelle, Chris, Diana, Jennifer, Judy, Lyn, Meghan, Melissa, Monica, Pam, Ruth, Sharon, Stephanie, Teresa, and Ursula.

The yarn for the Baby Blanket, my Shortcut Blanket and my Scenic Route Blankets was supplied by the lovely folks at Bendigo Woollen Mills. Thank you so much to the team for your ongoing support of my crochet designing.

Thank you to Tex Yarns for supplying the yarn for Kim's Scenic Route Blanket. It really is a stunning mix of colours and adds a wonderful sample to The Cove.

Lastly, but certainly not least, I want to express my gratitude to you who will set off on the path of your choosing to create something wonderful. Your support and excitement about The Cove kept me going when I felt like I would never get it done.

I hope that The Cove will be a fun crochet adventure for you, no matter which path you choose.

xx Shelley

About the Author

Shelley Husband is a designer, author, and serious supporter of making crocheting easy and enjoyable. While Shelley learned crocheting as a child, it took her almost 40 years to crochet her next granny square — and she hasn't stopped since.

Soon after that square, Shelley realised she had a new design in mind, and then another, and… well, let's just say, there's no slowing the new designs that continue to have her granny square community buzzing.

From her first book, Granny Square Flair, winning UK's Best Crochet Book in 2019, to a total tally of ten books, Shelley enjoys giving her community what they want. Now with an App, online group, and regular workshops across the country, Shelley loves getting the curious hooked on granny squares!

Old and new crocheters fall in love with the way Shelley designs patterns to be practical to grow their crochet confidence, one square at a time.

When Shelley's not running a retreat, working a workshop, or designing the next book from her hook, she's enjoying the land she loves and lives on in Gunditjmara Country (also known as Narrawong in Southwest Victoria, Australia).

If you haven't joined her community already, and you are crochet curious, you're most welcome to look her up on her website at shelleyhusbandcrochet.com.

Other Books

Granny Square Academy

Learn all there is to know about making granny squares, including how to read patterns.

Granny Square Academy 2

Expand your granny square knowledge with instructions for more advanced stitches and techniques.

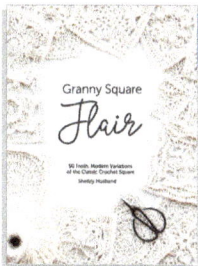

Granny Square Flair

50 written and charted granny square patterns and 11 project ideas to make with them.

Beneath the Surface

A beginner friendly pattern, with lots of extra support including video links.

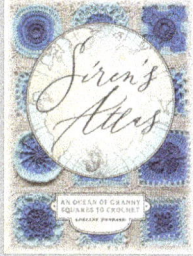

Siren's Atlas

64 written and charted granny square patterns for adventurous crocheters.

Granny Square Patchwork

40 written and charted granny squares patterns of 6 sizes and 12 projects to make with them.

Dotty Spotty

Classic circle-to-square granny square fun.

Nimue Crochet Blanket

A crochet quest of epic proportions with very detailed help including video links.

Corners and Curves

45 Granny Square patterns for crocheters ready to play with colours, corners and curves.

Buy my books direct in my online shop or at most online book retailers around the world. Visit my pattern shop for digital patterns galore.

shop.shelleyhusbandcrochet.com